10/15/79

To Brother & Sister

Norval A. Clay

Best Wishes

V.P. Black

Sermons for

THIS CROOKED GENERATION

By
V. P. Black, B.A., L.L.D.

Order From
Alabama Christian College
5345 Atlanta Highway
Montgomery, Alabama 36109

Published By
Parchment Press
Birmingham, Alabama 35208

ISBN 0-88428-032-2
Library of Congress Catalog Card Number: 74-76461

PRINTED IN THE UNITED STATES OF AMERICA

DEDICATION

To the administration, faculty, students and
friends of Alabama Christian
College

INTRODUCTION

V. P. Black was born in Lamar County, Alabama, December 15, 1918. He is one of ten boys who were reared on a dirt farm and knew the hard times of the depression.

He was self-supporting from the time he entered high school. His week-end preaching appointments made it possible for him to attend Freed-Hardeman College. Later in life he earned the B. A. degree at Alabama Christian College and was awarded the L. L. D. degree by the Alabama Christian School of Religion.

He married Lorrine Tennison of Booneville, Mississippi, on December 21, 1941. They have a son, Van P. Black, Jr., and a daughter, Becky Black Norton.

V. P. Black determined early in life to dedicate his life to preaching the gospel and has never lost sight of his goal. He began his full-time preaching ministry with the church in Booneville, Mississippi, in 1938. After working four years with that church, he moved to Avon Park, Florida, where he labored for two years. Since 1944, he has worked with the Plateau church in Mobile, Alabama. He has often remarked that one of the hardest goals for him to reach was to have 35 in attendance on Wednesday night his first year at Plateau. Today that great congregation is one of the strongest in the brotherhood. No church has been more committed to evangelism and Christian education.

For more than two decades V. P. Black has been widely sought after for evangelistic meetings. He has spoken in campaigns in Alabama, Georgia, Mississippi, North Carolina and other places. In 1965 when the churches on the Gulf Coast rented the new civic auditorium in Mobile for a campaign, they asked brother Black to be the speaker even though he had been a local minister in Mobile for over twenty years. The campaign resulted in 98 baptisms and 169 restorations. Meeting calls became so numerous that in 1970 brother Black began to devote full-time to meeting work as the evangelist of the Plateau church. He now conducts more than 40 meetings each year.

Even though brother Black claims to dislike writing, he is the author of a book of evangelist sermons, **We persuade Men.** He is also the author of four widely used books on stewardship, **My God and My Money; Rust As A Witness; Giving Our Way to Prosperity; Lord Teach Us How To Give.**

V. P. Black has lectured on stewardship more than any other man in the church. Hundreds of thousands of his books on stewardship have been used to great profit by over a thousand congregations. He has appeared on the lecture programs of almost all of our Christian colleges. On many occasions he has been the featured speaker on these programs.

V. P. Black has never forgotten what Christian education has meant to his life. Since 1960 he has dedicated himself to the promotion of Alabama Christian College. He has driven thousands of miles, spoken on hundreds of occasions, spent thousands of hours in deliberation, and given generously of his own money to support this college. All of his work has been donated because of his love for the school. He is a member of the Board of Directors and serves without remuneration as the Vice President for Development.

You will be deeply moved when you read these sermons as have the many thousands who have heard them in person.

E. R. Brannan
President
Alabama Christian College
1974

TABLE OF CONTENTS

THIS CROOKED GENERATION

This Lecture Delivered at David Lipscomb College in 1973.

INTRODUCTION

"And with many other words did he testify and exhort, saying, Save yourselves from this crooked generation." Acts 2:40. Let us look at this sermon that Peter preached and see how it is made up, that we may appreciate the statement, "Save yourselves from this untoward or crooked generatin." This sermon that Peter preached on the first Pentecost after the resurrection of Christ was full of scripture, and no sermon is worth listening to in this twentieth century unless it is full of scripture. The reason so much of our preaching is powerless and pointless is because so many sermons are not impregnated with the inspired word of God. Peter did not make this sermon; he quoted David and Joel and Psalms and the prophets and by inspiration set these quotations in their right relations to what had just happened in Jerusaiem and while he was talking history, he made history.

This sermon that Peter preached was full of Christ; if Christ had not lived it could not have been delivered. From beginning to end it palpatates with the duty and the glory of the Son of God. It is also full of holy unction. It was not delivered as a school boy might deliver a message. The great strong, rough frame of the fisherman, no doubt, trembled, quivered and vibrated by the great message that the tongue was delivering by inspiration. Without art or trick or mechanical skill this great man of God cried out and said, "Save yourselves from this crooked generation."

Many of those people were so pricked in their hearts that they did save themselves from that crooked generation. They did not applaud Peter; they were concerned about themselves. They were not pleased, but they were pierced. They were not gratified, but were convicted. They sought for no excuse and for no pleader to state their case. They simply wanted to know what to do to be saved from that crooked generation.

"Crooked" or "untoward" is said of anything which will not go toward or straight onward but will go now on this side, now on that, making a crooked path. The beast that rebels against the hand of its driver, pushes now in this direction and then in that direction, instead of that in which he is supposed to go. The serpent crawls along, never in a straight line but from this side to that side. The man who knows not his road takes a path now to the right hand now to the left hand, and goes not straight forward. The drunkard reels and staggers from side to side instead of going forward. All these are examples of untowardness or crookedness.

The commandments of God never lead in crooked ways but always straight forward. The transgressor is not found in the straight path but the crooked one. The transgressor has the willfulness and rebellion of the beast that will not be driven. He is a close follower of the crooked ways of the old serpent and walks in the mire of his sin. He is ignorant and blind and prefers the crooked ways. The transgressor is often drunk with pride and evil desires and cannot keep the straight path of godliness while in this sinful condition. Such is the character of a crooked generation. In the crooked generation are found the drunkard, the unchaste, the swearer, the thief, the covenant breaker; not only these, but all who hold the truth of God in unrighteousness.

I. WE ARE LIVING IN A CROOKED POLITICAL WORLD

When Gibbons wrote the history of the rise and fall of the Roman Empire, he gave five contributing factors that led to the fall of Rome.

1. Rapid increase of divorce, with the undermining of the sanctity of the home, which is the basic of society.
2. Higher and higher taxes; the spending of public money for bread and celebrations.
3. The mad craze for pleasure; sports becoming every year more exciting and more brutal.
4. The building of gigantic armaments, when the real enemy was within; the decadence of the people.
5. The decay of religion; faith fading into mere form, losing touch with life, and becoming impotent to guide it.

I have never read anything in my life that describes America more than these words. Every few days we read of graft and corruption in our government. We are living in an age when the poor are heavily taxed and many millionaires go free. We are living in an age when many believe that might makes right. We are living in an age when we see the strong overcome the weak and reek their passions upon them. We are living in an age when we see strong armies marching through the lands of the poor and unfortunate, burning, murdering and destroying until our soul is sick and we cry, "How long, and why does this happen?"

II. WE ARE LIVING IN A CROOKED MORAL GENERATION

America was founded by people who had strong religious and moral convictions. After almost two hundred years of existence we have become, in many ways, the most wicked nation of modern civilization. A description of America is found in Romans 1:20-32.

> For the invisible things of him from the creation of the world are clearly seen, being understood by the things that are made, even his eternal power and Godhead; so that they are without excuse: Because that, when they knew God, they glorified him not as God, neither were thankful; but became vain in their imaginations, and their foolish heart was darkened. Professing themselves to be wise, they became fools, And changed the glory of the uncorruptible God into an image made like to corruptible man, and to birds, and fourfooted beasts, and creeping things. Wherefore God also gave them up to uncleanness through the lusts of their own hearts, to dishonour their own bodies between themselves: Who changed the truth of God into a lie, and worshipped and served the creature more than the Creator, who is blessed for ever. Amen. For this cause God gave them up into vile affections: for even their women did change the natural use into that which is against nature: And likewise also the men, leaving the natural use of women, burned in their lust one toward another; men with men working that which is unseemly, and receiving in themselves that recompence of their error which was meet. And even as they did not like to retain God in their knowledge, God gave them over to a reprobate mind, to do those things which are not convenient; Being filled with all unrighteousness, fornication, wickedness, covetousness, maliciousness; full of envy, murder, debate, deceit, malignity; whisperers, backbiters, haters of God, despiteful, proud, boasters, inventors of evil things, disobedient to parents, without understanding, covenant breakers, without natural affection, implacable, unmerciful: Who knowing the judgment of God, that they which commit such things are worthy of death, not only do the same, but have pleasure in them that do them.

We also read in 2 Tim. 3:1-8 the following:

> This know also, that in the last days perilous times shall come, for men shall be lovers of their own selves, covetous, boaster, proud, blasphemers, disobedient to parents, unthankful, unholy, without natural affection, truce-breakers, false accusers, incontinent, fierce, despisers of those that are good, traitors, heady, highminded, lovers of pleasures more than lovers of God; having a form of godliness, but

denying the power thereof; from such turn away. For of this sort are they which creep into houses, and lead captive silly women laden with sins, led away with divers lusts, ever learning, and never able to come to the knowledge of the truth. Now as Jannes and Jambres withstood Moses, so do these also resist the truth: men of corrupt minds, reprobate concerning the faith.

With this sinful condition and only 6% of the world's population we boast of owning:
1.   40% of the world's silver.
2.   50% of the world's gold.
3.   60% of the world's copper.
4.   60% of the world's oil.
5.   40% of the world's railroads.
6.   85% of the world's automobiles.
7.   50% of the world's electricity.
8.   25% of the world's steel.

All of these material blessings have made us a proud, arrogant, defiant nation of people. In America there are over 37,000,000 children who are not receiving any kind of religious training. Almost half of the homes in America do not have a complete Bible. Very often I read where some one is pleading for money to send Bibles to some heathen nation. I do not object to this, in fact I approve; but somebody needs to be taking up money to put Bibles in the homes of this heathen nation that is known as America.

Illegitimacy has increased in America 300% in the last ten years. Our crime rate is increasing 11 times faster than our population. Last year we spent over fifty-one billion dollars on crime. Many of our policemen are complaining that when they make an arrest, they are likely to turn the criminal loose and try the policeman.

The sales of pornographic books, magazines and films in the United States are estimated to reach two billion dollars per year. There are 89,623 more taverns than church buildings, temples, mosques and synagogues combined in our country. There are 410,692 taverns compared to 321,069 religious meeting places.

There is a serious crime committed every 7 seconds, a violent crime every 48 seconds, a murder every 36 minutes, a robbery every 2 minutes, a forcible rape every 14 minutes, an aggravated assault every 2 minutes, an automobile theft every 36 seconds, a grand larceny every

21 seconds, a suicide every 23 minutes. Shoplifters cost merchants two billion dollars this past Christmas. We are living in an age when righteousness is winked at and law is defied.

As we face these cold brutal facts we must remember that God has said: "Righteousness exalteth a nation; but sin is a reproach to any people." Prov. 14:34. "The wicked shall be turned into hell, and all the nations that forget God." Ps. 9:17. If there was ever a time when we need to teach every father, mother, son and daughter (Phil. 2:15) that time is now, and the verse says: "That ye may be blameless and harmless, the sons of God, without rebuke in the midst of a crooked and perverse nation, among whom ye shine as lights in the world."

I am convinced, in my own mind, that America cannot stand much longer if this terrible tide of wickedness continues to sweep over America. In years gone by God has destroyed every nation that reached a certain point of wickedness. God must destroy his enemies that right may be triumphant over wrong, good over evil, God over satan.

Let us look at the history of the world. After man lived upon the earth for about sixteen hundred years, we read in Gen. 6:6,7 "And it repented the Lord that he had made man on the earth, and it grieved him at his heart. And the Lord said, I will destroy man whom I have created from the face of the earth; both man, and beast, and creeping thing, and the fowls of the air; for it repenteth me that I have made them."

Let us look at Sodom and Gomorrah. Gen. 19:24-25 "Then the Lord rained upon Sodom and upon Gomorrah brimstone and fire from the Lord out of heaven; And he overthrew those cities, and all the plain, and all the inhabitants of the cities, and that which grew upon the ground."

When God was fed up with the Egyptians, He destroyed them. Ex. 14:28 "And the waters returned, and covered the chariots, and the horsemen, and all the host of Pharaoh that came into the sea after them; there remained not so much as one of them." Even the proud city of Jerusalem was destroyed when she reached a certain point of wickedness. America is one of the most wicked nations of the world today. It could very well be that, unless there are enough Christian people who can to some appreciable degree hold back this terrible tide of wickedness, God may rise up some mighty nation like Red China or Russia and bring America to her knees. It is true, I do not know what the future holds but I know who holds the future.

III. WHAT WILL HAPPEN TO THE CHURCH
IN THIS CROOKED GENERATION?

If there was ever a time when preachers need to preach the plain simple truths of the Bible that time is now. We need to make the plea that Jeremiah made in Jer. 6:16: "Thus saith the Lord, Stand ye in the ways, and see, and ask for the old paths, where is the good way, and walk therein, and ye shall find rest for your souls. But they said, We will not harken."

Because of the sinful condition of the world it makes it more difficult for the church to remain sound. I am convinced that television has done more to demoralize America and modernize the church than any one thing since Pentecost.

A parent-teacher association in Chicago has become so angrily aware of the influence of television on their children, that they appointed thirty sets of parents to monitor the programs of four Chicago stations, and this is what they found that took place in one week's time:

1. 93 murders had been fed to their children.
2. There were 275 crimes of violence in 134 children's programs.
3. The children saw:

   a. 78 Shootings
   b. 9 Kidnapings
   c. 9 Robberies
   d. 44 Gunfights
   e. 33 Sluggings
   f. 2 Knifings
   g. 3 Whiplashings
   h. 2 Poisonings
   i. 2 Bombings

4. The gory programs ran from 9 a.m. to children's bedtime.

We should take the boards where we post the attendance and contribution and post the following: "Your child this last week may have seen 78 shootings, 9 kidnapings, 9 robberies, 44 gunfights, 33 sluggings, 2 knifings, 3 whiplashings, 2 poisonings, 2 bombings."

A code for the use of television has recently been published in six British newspapers. The highlights of the code are:

1. Children should not watch television more than 2 hours a day.
2. Horror programs should be forbidden by any age.
3. Parents should agree beforehand on programs they consider suitable for their children.
4. Parents and teachers should protest objectionable programs and commend producers for worthwhile programs. All of these are a part of the crooked generation in which we live.

The church is faced with social liberalism in this crooked generation. When Paul wrote to Timothy instructing him what to teach, he had these words of admonition: (I Tim. 2:9-10) "In like manner also, that women adorn themselves in modest apparel, with shamefacedness and sobriety; not with braided hair, or gold, or pearls, or costly array; but which becometh women professing godliness with good works." It is evident that the fashion world has lost all sense of decency in regard to ladies clothing. I want to say in defence of the teenagers in the Lord's church that most of them are innocent and do not realize all the dangers involved in dressing skimpily (there are exceptions of course). The parents are to be blamed for not teaching the teenager.

I read of a father who impressed me. His daughter came home angry and excited and told her parents how a man had insulted her. The girl and mother demanded that the father do something about it. He did. He called the girl into another room and said, "Darling, let me tell you a thing or two that will help you see this matter in the proper perspective. You are young and attractive, and your new short dress displays the beauty of your body. Your arms are bare to the shoulders and the low cut of your blouse leave little to the imagination. Your skirts are scant and narrow and your hemlines are such that modesty is hard to maintain when you are standing and impossible when you are seated.

"I have talked with you before, my daughter, about the nature of men and boys. So, you knew better than to dress as such. You obviously did not present a picture of a careful, dedicated Christian girl. Had you done so, you would have received the careful, considerate and respectful treatment usually given to the obviously Christian woman."

The Bible was written for all people in every country and climate, for every century as long as time lasts. The Holy Spirit has given us a message that each generation can understand and apply to everyday living. Human nature is the same in all ages. Customs may and do change but principles of righteousness do not change.

The apostle Paul tells women to adorn themselves in modest apparel, and this is to be done in all ages. The word "adorn," defind by Webster, is to "beautify, dignify, ornament, embellish." McKnight says: "The Greek word 'adorn' signifies not only what is beautiful, but what is neat and clean, and suitable to one's station."

An article from a daily newspaper in Toronto, Canada carried the following article. "Ninty-one percent of Toronto's policemen think a woman in a 'revealing miniskirt' is more likely to be a rape victim than is her more modest sister, a spokeman for the Toronto force said Tuesday." "Since 1964, the year the mini was introduced to the female fashion market, rapes have increased by 68 percent in the United States and 90 percent in England," said a law officer in a police publication.

Paul Harvey, a noted writer and commentator has recently said on one of his daily broadcasts the following; "Professional law enforcement official in 50 states were asked, 'Does the short skirt invite sex crime?' 92% said yes. Where forcible rape is now our nation's fastest increasing crime, a separate category of 'molestation of young girls' is also increasing at a record rate." Mary Quant, London designer, mother of the miniskirt, said on November 13, 1967, "Miniclothes are symbolic of those girls who want to seduce a man . . ." and, as if to confirm her conclusion, the years the skirts went up, crimes against women demonstrated a parallel increase. The only nudist we read about in the New Testament is the maniac that Christ healed. Mark 5:1-15.

The church is faced with doctrinal liberalism in this crooked generation. Liberalism, in all probability, is the greatest danger facing the Lord's church. We have been reading a great deal about situation ethics in recent years. We must remember that the Bible condemns lying, sodomy, homosexuality and adultry and no situation ethics can make these things right.

Many of the liberals, as they would state the case, are reacting against the spirit of legalism which, according to them, has prevailed in the church a long time. These men may be described as anti-legalists. These liberal brethren are set for the defence of a relevent social gospel, and they are very critical of the "five steppers" within the church—that is those of us who teach the truth concerning the plan of salvation, by teaching that an alien sinner must (1) hear the gospel, (2) believe on Christ's Son, (3) repent of his sins, (4) confess his faith in Christ, and (5) be baptized into Christ for the remission of his sins. These men would have us to believe that the Holy Spirit works in the Christian above and separate from and independent of the word of God.

These "Holy Spirit directed" anti-legalists claimed to have spoken in tongues, received revelations and performed miracles. They often turn out the lights during the religious service so that they can better "feel the presence of the Holy Spirit." They talk of how the "Spirit of God was present in such a great way." They seem to be far more interested in the communication they receive directly from the Holy Spirit than they are in the communication they received from the word of God which was given by the Holy Spirit.

Many of these liberals are attempting to undermine the authority of the scripture by calling in question the integrity, genuineness and authenticity of the scripture. Many of these men are found in high positions of influence, and it seems that they feel a burden, often a passion, to break the influence of the word of God. With them truth is only relative; with them there is no truth, except relative truth; there are no absolutes, except relative absolutes; and there is no righteousness, except relative righteousness.

Many of these liberals in the church are beginning to band together in small groups in some of our cities as if they were some kind of brain trust for the Lord's church. These liberals are apostates from the truth of God and they must be marked. The apostle John includes this crowd when he said, "If there come any unto you, and bring not this doctrine, receive him not into your house, neither bid him God speed: For he that biddeth him God speed is a partaker of his evil deeds," 2 John 10-11. In John 8:32 we read, "And ye shall know the truth, and the truth shall make you free."

REACHING THE MASSES WITH THE GOSPEL

This lecture delivered at Abilene Christian College,
Abilene, Texas in 1969.

God in his divine wisdom planned and worked for 4000 years before bringing the church of Christ into existence. He gave a divine and perfect plan for the church.

The church of Christ has a perfect founder, foundation, and head. He is Jesus Christ the Prince of Peace and Priest of the Most High God. Jesus Christ proved himself to be the son of God by going with the pale monarch of death into the silent darkness of the grave and while there he broke his crown and took the keys of death and rode aloft to heaven and shouted as he went through the air, "I have the keys of death, hell and the grave in my hands."

We need to impress upon the minds of the people the urgent need of reaching the masses with the gospel. In the 20th century there is still an urgent need for simple New Testament teaching. Where men were once in a fog of confusion due to sectarianism, strife, and bitterness, they are in a denser fog today, produced by philosophies, theories, and confusion confounded. Hundreds of cults, social up-lift schemes, and materialistic propaganda thrust themselves upon the scene until men despair of knowing where to seek the truth. Many of these people turn to cynic indifference and fill their lives with worldly pleasures.

Men are weary with confusion and darkness, but endure it because they have never seen the light. There are millions of people who are now indifferent to Christ and his gospel, who would gladly obey the gospel if they could come to know the simple truths contained therein. With this New Testament message so badly needed, we cannot, we must not let sectarianism and bitterness become so strong that God's people will divide into camps so antagonistic that Christ will be put to shame and his church become stagnant.

People in the religious world are sick and tired of hearing ministers quote from 20th century philosophers instead of the apostles during the first century. People are weary of ministers quoting from newspapers and magazines instead of quoting from the New Testament. Unless we carry the same gospel message to the people of this age that Christ and his apostles carried to them during the first century, then all our efforts are vain.

We must recognize the fact that a social gospel will not save the world. It may tickle the ear and appeal to man's pride but in reality it is as sounding brass or a tinkling symbol. A moral gospel won't save man from his sins. The best moral man that ever lived has committed enough sins to separate him from God for eternity. A ceremonial gospel won't save. One could live to be as old as Methuselah and obey to perfection every ceremonial law devised by man but unless he contacts the blood of Christ, he has no hope offered him in the word of God. Christ by His shed blood made it possible for us to be saved. We must preach Christ crucified, with his own sweat and blood creeping from his tender brow, dripping from his hands and feet, gushing from his side, telling us that all the blood of all the animals of the world can never take away the sin of the world.

In this age when many are preaching a socialistic gospel, others a moral gospel, some a ceremonial gospel, and still others an ethical gospel, we must emphasize the gospel of the blood. We must preach this gospel because it has power to effect a reconciliation between sinner and God. Because it shows how the interest of all sinners was aimed at in the death of Christ. Because it proves that through the blood of Christ the sinner can be washed and made as white as the driven snow.

> For whosoever shall call upon the name of the Lord shall be saved. How then shall they call on him in whom they have not believed? and how shall they believe in him of whom they have not heard? and how shall they hear without a preacher? And how shall they preach, except they be sent? as it is written, How beautiful are the feet of them that preach the gospel of peace, and bring glad tidings of good things! (Rom. 10:13-15).

When Paul wrote this epistle, the ancient Roman virtue, the admirable simplicity, and the unconquerable courage had died away. With these things also died the old religion. The decay and corruption of it were accelerated by the engrafting of new and dark superstition. The change in social life was startling and vice was defied. The pagan world knew not God. The sound of the gospel had gone forth and its influence upon their lives was startling. This gospel modified private individuals, social and state life.

Nations where this gospel has not been preached have been found practicing self-torments, devil worship, human sacrifices, and slaughter of wives. They practice constant wars, vendetta, slavery, polygamy, degradation of women, superstitions of priestcraft and witchcraft. But when the gospel of peace reaches the people it sheds light and ends fear.

This gospel that is to be carried to the masses is a report. A report that is divine in origin, unique in its character, authentic in its facts, authoritative in its statements, and marvelous in its declaration.

This gospel reports about a most wonderful love. "For God so loved the world, that he gave his only begotten Son, that whosoever believeth in him shall not perish, but have everlasting life." (John 3:16). Here we have a volume in a verse, an ocean in a dewdrop, a hemisphere of light in solitary luminary, and eternity of mystery and mercy! Eternity cannot exhaust its wealth of interest and wonderment! The greatest love story known to man is the love that God has for Adam's lost and recreant race.

This gospel reports on the life of Christ, the life of Christ which the gospel makes known, has no parallel in the history of races. The mysterious conception was grandly confirmed by his mysterious career; unique in birth, he was unique all through. If one link in the chain can be found faulty, then the whole chain is faulty. But every link has been found a perfect link; his whole life wonderously consistent, complete, and unrivaled. For more than nineteen hundred years this life has been stirring humanity to its very core and center. In philosophy he is the mightiest enigma! In the universe he is the highest attraction! In life he is the inimitable ideal. In the world he is the absolute ruler. From that wonderful life, as from a fountain of eternity, has flowed vital truths of freshness, beauty and blessedness wherever they have gone.

This gospel reports most wonderful provisions: provisions of mercy and of merit to avert the penal blow and cancel the guilt; of merit to redignify the acquitted rebel and reinstate him in God's eternal favor; provisions equal to the demands of one soul or a world of souls enough for each, enough for all, enough forevermore. There is multiplied grace, goodness and glory; there is a variety so great, a fullness so vast, a supply so magnificent and princely that the roll of unceasing ages will fail to exhaust either the one or the other. The gospel of Christ reports wonderful results. Obedient to the imperial summons of the master to, "go in the world and preach the gospel to every creature" the apostles and their co-laborers, these giants of the cross, embarked on their sublime but hazardous enterprise; beginning at Jerusalem, they sailed forth to regions beyond and preached Jesus and the resurrection. In less than fifty years after they started the gospel had sounded its report all over the Roman empire, and even in the ranks of Caesar's household.

This gospel eclipses all others, and stands out with a singularity and supremacy at once unprecedented and divine; reporting as it reveals and revealing as it reports Jehovah's mind and will, the sympathy and benevolence of his great heart, before which multitudes have bowed in reverence and submission. View it in what light you may—as a remedy, a revelation, a message, a system or history—it reports results most astounding and sublime. It is so simple that a child may understand it; yet so deep that philosophers can never fathom its depth. So cheap that it can be had for the asking; so precious that millions cannot buy it. So full that it can never be diminished; so universal that none is outside its possible benedictions.

Our mission is to carry the gospel to the masses. "The fruit of the righteous is a tree of life; and he that winneth souls is wise." (Prov. 11:30). "And they that be wise shall shine as the brightness of the firmament; and they that turn many to righteousness as the stars forever and ever." (Dan. 13:3). We live in a world of sin and sinners and it is our duty to rescue those who are lost. Jails and prisons are crowded with criminals and the air is reeking with blasphemy. We are living in an age when more homage is paid to gold than to goodness. Go to the United Nations headquarters and there you hear only wrangling and argumentative speeches. We read of armies that rush to battle in a den of noise and in a cloud of smoke; blood flows and indescribable misery follows. We read of the strong overcoming the weak and wreaking their passions upon them, we read of cruel might marching through lands burning, murdering, and ravishing until our soul is sickened and we turn away and cry, "All of this because of sin."

The only remedy for this sin-sick world is the gospel. The church has the responsibility of carrying the gospel to these people. The task assigned to the church is this matter of evangelization is no light one. So great is this task that we have no time to argue over the time of day we should partake of the Lord's Supper, whether one must kneel or stand while praying, or to what degree the Holy Spirit dwells in the child of God. We also need to stop arguing over how to carry the gospel to the world; we just need to get busy and do it.

We hear much about theories of inspiration, theories of atonement, theories of faith, theories of the Holy Spirit and theories of the indwelling spirit. Oh God, hasten the day when we will accept the plain simple truths of thy word and then obey them. Regardless of all the claims we may make, unless the mighty working power of God is demonstrated in our lives by carrying his gospel to all parts of the world and by clothing the naked and feeding the hungry, we have no right to exist. The church was not established to entertain or to amuse the world but to save it; not to mock the world but to redeem it through Christ. When our pulpits become occupied with men who have a tongue of orthodoxy and a heart of heterodoxy, we will lose our identity; and when the church loses its distinctiveness, it has lost its power. Christ, the head of the church, continually walks among us, saying, "What do ye more than others?" It is only when we do more than others that we become a peculiar or a distinctive people. We have not begun, in the true sense of the word, to serve God until we do more than others; until we learn to work, sacrifice and put the Kingdom of God first, we are no more than baptized pagans.

World evangelization began with a company of only twelve men which grew into a church of three thousand the first day. In a generation churches were planted all over the Roman empire and the gospel became known to the world. The mission of the church is to turn the world from darkness to light, to convert a sin-lost and sin-ruined world from error, to lead them by the truth, the gospel, into the Kingdom, the church, of our Lord and Master. This the church must do if it is to carry out the purpose of God our Father and Christ our Saviour.

The church would cease to exist in a generation if it were not for missions. We ourselves, whether we admit it and thank God for it or deny it, are the fruit of missions. Our forebears were naked savages. The gospel of Christ has made us what we are. Christianity is essentially a missionary system. Missions inhere in the gospel just as heat does in fire or cold in ice or as light in the sun. One congregation located in the city of Antioch (Syria) in the long ago sent out a missionary in the person of the apostle Paul. During Paul's stay with this church he taught them their duty in preaching the gospel to others. This great church sent Paul on one missionary journey, then a second and a third one; and, as a result of these journeys and this one church, congregations were established in Perga, Antioch, Pisidia, Iconium, Lystra, Derbe, Philippi, Ephesus, Thessalonica, Corinth and possibly many other places. These established congregations became radiating centers for the gospel. "For from you sounded out the word of the Lord not only in Macedonia and Achaia but also in every place your faith to God-ward is spread abroad; so that we need not to speak anything." (I Thess. 1:8). "And this continued by the space of two years; so that all they which dwelt in Asia heard the word of the Lord Jesus, both Jews and Greeks." (Acts 19:10).

The average congregation may be described by various adjectives, but one that does not exactly fit it is "evangelistic." This condition of being unevangelistic exists in spite of the fact that Christ has placed upon it the responsibility of preaching the gospel to every creature. In spite of all our pretensions, the average church is far from being evangelistic. The brethren meet and sing a few songs, have a prayer, study a lesson, have the Lord's Supper, take up the half-hearted offering and hear a sermon. Occasionally there is a gospel meeting consisting of eight days and few souls are saved. The Lord's day morning service, usually the best attended service, is more formal than evangelistic, with very little time devoted to the preaching that God has ordained to bring sinners to repentance.

Is it possible there are many among us who do not know the church exists primarily to convert sinners to Christ? For instance, ask any child why the fire department exists, and he will tell you to fight fires. Why do we have doctors? To help people get well. Why do we have policemen? To put bad people in jail. Why does the church exist? The chances are he will not say, "The church exists to snatch souls out of hell and to help sin-sick souls to get right with God." Why will he not answer correctly about the purpose of the church? It is because we are not emphasizing evangelism very fervently. To solve this problem we must have compassion for souls.

> But when he saw the multitudes, he was moved with compassion on them, because they fainted, and were scattered abroad, as sheep having no shepherd. Then saith he unto his disciples, The harvest truly is plenteous, but the labourers are few: Pray ye therefore the Lord of the harvest, that he will send forth labourers into his harvest. (Mat. 9:36-38).

If we are going to be successful in converting sinners, it will take more than a meaningless sermonette delivered in a dry-eyed manner. Those who play on the stage use the expression "sympathetic identification" to indicate that they have studied the character in question so carefully that they are able to act as the other would under similar circumstances. We need to sense deeply the need of those around us who are living without Christ.

> I say the truth in Christ, I lie not, my conscience also bearing me witness in the Holy Ghost. That I have great heaviness and continual sorrow in my heart. For I could wish that myself were accursed from Christ for my brethren, my kinsmen according to the flesh. (Rom. 9:1-3). The Lord is not slack concerning his promise, as some men

count slackness; but is long suffering to us-ward, not willing that any should perish, but that all should come to repentance. (II Pet. 3:9). Let him know, that he which converteth the sinner from the error of his way, shall save a soul from death, and shall hide a multitude of sins. (James 5:20). And others save with fear, pulling them out of the fire; hating even the garment spotted by the flesh. (Jude 23).

Contrary to the things that we have pointed out from the New Testament, the lives of many professed Christians are spiritually "dry and parched." Whole churches, in some instances, are satisfied to go through with some meaningless, dry-eyed perfunctory thing they call a worship service. While all around them, or sometime in their very midst, there are sinners who are not rebuked. The preacher in this pulpit is unlike the Christ whom he claims to serve.

To reach the masses with the gospel we must be zealous. If we are not zealous we will become like the church in Laodicea. This church was lukewarm about everything. It was dying as churches can die, of moderation and respectability. It may, in its apparently sound and safe prosperity, have been envied by other churches; nobody in the church brought any disgrace upon the Christian name. The church did not make the holy and inspiring witness of consistency in keeping things at a high spiritual level. It was unconcerned, indifferent, content to go on, aiming at nothing and doing nothing. The lukewarm are neither earnest for God, nor utterly indifferent to religion. They are perhaps best described as those who take an interest in religion, but whose worship of their idol of good taste, or good form, leads them to regard enthusiasm as ill-bred and disturbing. Those people have never put themselves to any inconvenience, braved any reproach, or abandoned any comfort for the cause of Christ, but hope to keep well with the world, while they flatter themselves that they stand well with God. Carlyle calls this, "The hypocrisy that does not know itself to be hypocritical."

The people of Laodicea were not cold, but they were not hot; they were not infidels, but they were not earnest belivers; they did not oppose the gospel, neither did they defend it; they were not working mischief, neither were they doing any great good; they were not disreputable in moral character, but they were not distinguished for holiness; they were not irreligious, but they were not enthusiastic in piety nor eminent for zeal. They were what the world calls "moderates," they were of the broad-church school, they were neither bigots nor Puritans, they were prudent and avoided fanaticism. Respectable and adverse to excitement, these people, no doubt, had prayer meetings but there were few present for they liked quiet evenings at home. When more attended, the meetings were still very dull, for they did their praying very deliberately and were afraid of getting too excited. It would have been an easy thing for such a church to consider vigor, zeal, and enthusiasm as being vulgar.

Such churches have Bible classes and all sorts of agencies; but they might as well be without them, for no energy is displayed and no good comes of them. They have elders and deacons who are excellent pillars of the church, if the chief work of pillars is to sit still and exhibit no motion or emotion. These churches have ministers but their wings have been closely clipped, for they do not fly very far in preaching the everlasting gospel; they may be shining lights of eloquence, but they are not burning lights of grace, setting men's hearts on fire.

These indifferent people are not so cold as to abandon the work, or to give up their meeting for prayer, or to reject the gospel; if they did so, then they could be convinced of their error and brought to repentance. Such people are not hot for truth, nor hot for conversion, nor hot for holiness; they are not "firey" enough to burn the stubble of sin, nor zealous enough to make Satan angry, nor fervent enough to make a living sacrifice for the cause of God. These people are like the amphibious animal that can live in water as well as on land. The half-hearted convert is one who can be at home in the world or in the church; one who can find pleasure in sin and also can find pleasure in hearing a sermon.

Men are less apt to repent when they are in the middle passage between hot and cold than if they were in the worst extremes of sin. If they are like Saul of Tarsus, enemies of God, they may be converted. But if like Gamaliel, they are neither opposing nor favoring, they will probably remain as they are till they die. Five thousand lukewarm members are only five thousand impediments in the church, but a dozen earnest, passionate spirits, determined to glorify Christ by winning souls to his cause are "more than conquerors." If God is worth serving at all he is worth serving with zeal. One needs a pure and fervent zeal to take his stand with the few, or even alone, if necessary, to cry out against sin and wickedness. Righteous zeal is powerful; it can no more remain silent in the presence of evil than a roaring lion in the presence of its prey or a mighty army in the presence of its enemies. Zeal will attack the walls of Jericho with a ram's horn or go against a giant with a shepherd's sling. The Christians of this generation have the responsibility of carrying the gospel to every person of this generation. Yes, our responsibilities are great and our time is limited.

UNPRECEDENTED OPPORTUNITIES
TO REEMPHASIZE THE
RESTORATION PLEA

This lecture delivered at David Lipscomb College, 1970.

The position we occupy in life depends upon the attitude we have toward opportunities that come our way. In science and in literature there are those who stand as giants among small men because they, while in raw youth, saw an opportunity and took hold of it. In the church of our Lord there have been those with very humble backgrounds and mean circumstances, but because they took advantage of opportunities that were passing by rose from obscurity to the distinction of being mighty powerful men of God.

When our Lord was upon the earth Jerusalem had her opportunities. She had been blessed with more prophets, teachers and reformers than any city of the world. In fact, it seems that Jerusalem was over-weight with privileges and opportunities, yet they neglected and despised again and again those opportunities and as a result of their indifference, they fell under the awful judgment of God.

God will not continue to grant us opportunities if we neglect those he has already given us. He did not give five more talents to the man who took his one and buried it.

It is a Bible proven truth that opportunities neglected will be taken away. Israel had the opportunity to go into the promised land but did not take advantage of it. The lesson we learn in the history of Israel is repeated by Christ more than once in his parables. In the parable of the wicked husbandmen, the Lord of the vineyard is represented as letting out his vineyard, "Unto other husbandmen, who shall render him the fruits in their seasons." (Mt. 21:41). We have the same truth in the parable of the talents, "Unto every one that hath shall be given . . but from that hath not shall be taken away even that which he hath." (Mt. 25:29). The history of the Jews is a solemn warning against the neglect of opportunities.

Since Peter stood and proclaimed God's message on the day of Pentecost, and since Paul stood on Mars Hill and proclaimed the truths of Jehovah and condemned their unknown gods, man has never had the opportunities to proclaim the gospel throughout the world as he now has in the latter part of the 20th Century.

With all these opportunities coming to us we must not forget to reemphasize the plea made by those great men of God during the Restoration movement. When preachers in the church of Christ know more about denominational preachers than they do the Restoration preachers, and when preachers quote more often from Barth, Trueblood, and Tillich than they do Paul, Peter and John, and when the sermons preached from our pulpits are filled with articles from magazines and newspapers instead of messages from the word of God, it should be a signal to all who love the truth to see the need of reemphasizing the plea made by Restoration preachers. Those who believe the scriptures thoroughly furnish a man unto salvation are tired of hearing ministers quote from magazines instead of quoting from the New Testament. They are sick of hearing preachers quote from philosophers instead of quoting from the apostles.

Our preaching today must be centered around the cross. A social gospel will not save the soul. It may tickle the ear and appeal to man's pride but in reality it is as, "sounding brass or a tinkling cymbal." We must preach Christ crucified with His own sweat and blood creeping from His tender brow, dripping from His hands and feet, gushing from His side, telling us that the blood of animals can never take away the sins of the world.

In this age when many are preaching a socialistic gospel, others a moral gospel, some a ceremonial gospel and still others an ethical gospel, we must emphasize the preaching of Christ and his blood.

Moses, fifteen hundred years before Pentecost, emphasized the coming of this Christ as one being like unto himself, a Mediator, Law-giver and Ruler. Israel's greatest poet spoke of the one who would sit on David's throne at the right hand of God. Daniel, standing among the ruins of ancient empires with the horoscope of time in his hand said: "In the days of these kings shall the God of heaven set up a Kingdom which shall not be left to other people, but it shall break in pieces and consume all these Kingdoms and it shall stand forever."

This King over this kingdom is our Conqueror and our Federal Representive. It's true he was taken down from the cross a bloody corpse and carried away to the grave. On this day hell shouted for joy, death waved her black banners in triumph, sighs ran along amid the bones of the patriarchs and a wail of woe was heard throughout the world. But on the third day our Lord broke open the gates of hell and came forth more powerful than Samson when he carried away the gates of Gaza. Marching in the greatness of his power to save, he proclaimed liberty to a captive world by saying, "I am he who was dead and am alive forever more and have in my hands the keys of death, hell and the grave."

In John 14:6, "Jesus saith unto him, I am the way, the truth, and the life: no man cometh unto the Father, but by me." This is the central, fundamental and crowning truth of the Bible. It is the master key that unlocks revelation's arcanum. It is the master hand which unravels its mysteries and weaves its disentangled threads into a beautiful web of consistent and comprehensible truth. It is the keystone hewn by our Emmanuel out of the diamond rocks of heaven, chiseled and polished by his artistic hand, while calvary trembled beneath the blows of the weighty hammer which awakened the dead and frightened created light back into the womb of darkness. And now this finished structure glitters in the symmetric arches of the beautiful bridge of salvation stretching from the regions of death to the regions of life, spanning hell and hades, with every stone cemented by the blood of its architect and builder.

Our brethren in every generation must be taught the great and fundamental truths upon which the church is built. In every generation we must emphasize and reemphasize the restoration plea made over a hundred years ago which shook the very foundation of denominationalism. If the time should ever come that we cease to reemphasize the restoration plea we will become just another denomination among hundreds that already exist.

WE MUST REEMPHASIZE THAT
TRUTH IS ABSOLUTE

We are living in an age when most preaching in the religious world and some in the Lord's church could be classified as Parson Gray's—a type preaching that is pleasant to saint and sinner alike: when sinners are not rebuked, the unfaithful are at ease, and those in doctrinal error are not shown wherein they are wrong. This type preaching is done because, we are told by a group that is now a minority in the church, truth is not absolute. Those who tell us truth is not absolute and that one must always search for the truth and will never be able to find it are described in I Tim. 3:7: "Ever learning, and never able to come to the knowledge of the truth."

Listen to Alexander Campbell, and I quote, "Often have I said, and often have I written, that truth, truth eternal and divine, is now, and long has been with me the pearl of great price. To her I will, with the blessing of God, sacrifice everything. But on no altar will I offer her a victim. If I have lost sight of truth, God who searcheth the heart knows I have not done it intentionally. With my whole heart I have sought the truth and I know I have found it. Numbers with me count nothing. Let God be true, and every man a liar. Let truth stand though the heavens fail." Alexander Campbell believed that truth was absolute and that it could be found by honest sincere seekers. With these positive and absolute truths taught by Campbell and his contemporaries the church of Christ had, in the year 1850, become the fourth largest religious body in America. Some have said that there were three reasons why the church of Christ grew so rapidly from 1850 to 1860:

1.   Those restoration preachers stood for something.
2.   They knew what they stood for.
3.   They had courage to carry out their convictions.

John 1:17, "For the law was given by Moses, but grace and truth came by Jesus Christ." The truth that Jesus taught was absolute truth, not relative truth. By hearing the truth and obeying truth the disciples of Christ were made free from sin. This knowledge was not just an intellectual grasp. Although it included this grasp it also included the experimental knowledge that comes through doing the truth. The final test of our knowledge is to be found in what we do. I John 2:3-4, "And hereby we know that we know him, if we keep his commandments. He that saith I know him, and keepeth not his commandments, is a liar and the truth is not in him."

Jesus did not mean that we know everything, but we can know enough truth to be made free and we can continue to study and learn and thereby grow in the knowledge of the truth. These absolute truths are just as important in this 20th century as in the first century. These truths are just as important because man's nature has not changed. There is not a person living that can name one new sin. If it were possible to go back to the ancient Babylonian civilization and see how they lived, we would find the same crimes, the same sins, the same heartaches, the same joys, which we see about us today. What the world needs today is the gospel of Christ plainly taught without subtractions, additions, or revision. Our responsibility is to preach it until the masses hear, until sinners repent, and hope that accountable people will obey it. This can only be accomplished by teaching the absolute truths of God.

Many of those great men in the restoration movement were well trained and well educated men who nobly defended the faith against sectarianism. They did not defend it as "Church of Christ doctrine." They believed that God's word is the truth that makes men free. (Jn. 8:32; Jn. 17:17). They believed that the only right way is the way set forth in the Bible. They believed that a person could be a Christian without being sectarian and that he could and did belong to the church of the Lord by the same process that he belonged to Christ. They believed that he could be a Christian without being a member of any denomination. These men believed in the plan of salvation set forth in the New Testament by which one is brought to an understanding of the will of God. These absolute truths preached led people who heard to believe, repent, confess Christ and to be baptized into Christ for the remission of their sins. One may sarcastically or disrespectfully or irreverently refer to these acts of obedience as "finger exercise" or those who teach these absolute truths as "five steppers". But, it is an absolute truth that these religious rebels are going to be judged by the very truth that they disrespect.

WE MUST REEMPHASIZE RESPECT
FOR AUTHORITY

America is sick today because there has been a breakdown of law and order. This breakdown of law and order had its origin in the religious world and has spilled over into the social, moral and political world. Hear with what authority the Bible speaks.

> Acts 3:22-23, For Moses truly said unto the fathers, a prophet shall the Lord your God raise up unto you of your brethren, like unto me; him shall ye hear in all things whatsoever he shall say unto you. And it shall come to pass, that every soul, which will not hear that prophet shall be destroyed from among the people. Mt. 7:29, For he taught them as one having authority, and not as the scribes. Mt. 28:19, And Jesus came and spoke unto them saying, All power or authority is given unto me in heaven and on earth. Jn. 3:26-27, For as the Father hath life in himself: so hath he given to the Son to have life in himself; and hath given him authority to execute judgment also, because he is the Son of man.

We should not argue with anything Christ has done or said! Man is prone to say within his own heart, "The Lord just doesn't know what he is talking about, or the Lord just doesn't understand my case." The Lord does know and the Lord does understand.

Peter was prone to question his Lord. In a vision, Peter saw heaven open, and a certain vessel descending unto him, as it had been a great sheet knit at the four corners, and let down to the earth, and wild beasts, and creeping things and fowls of the air. And there came a voice to him, rise, Peter: kill and eat. But Peter said, "Not so, Lord" for I have never eaten anything that is common or unclean. And the voice spoke unto him again the second time, what God hath cleansed, that call thou not common. (Acts 10). "Not so, Lord" was Peter's first reaction. Has this ever been our reaction to the command of God? Peter learned his lesson—never to question the Lord's authority!

We read in Eph. 1:21-22; Eph. 4:4; Eph. 5:23 and Mt. 16:19 that there is one church. How many react to this statement with a "Not so, Lord?" The Bible teaches baptism is for the remission of sin. How many say, "Not so Lord?"

Jeremiah warned his people. "Hearken not unto the words of the prophets that prophesy unto you: they make you vain: they speak a vision of their heart, and not out of the mouth of the Lord." (Jer. 23:16). Some today make it appear that they are speaking from the Bible, when in reality they are merely speaking visions of their heart. Such is a disrespect for the authority of God's word.

When Jeroboam was trying to get a following among the Israelites, he set up a god in Bethel, and another in Dan. Then he said, "It is too much for you to go to Jerusalem. Behold thy gods, O Israel, which brought thee up out of the land of Egypt." (I King 12:28). God said this thing became a sin (I Kings 12:30). It became a sin because it was outright rebellion against the authority of God's arrangement. We are hearing and reading of those who are in rebellion against what they call the "establishment." This is not a new thing, for this is what Jeroboam did. In reality his rebellion was against God.

The church of our Lord made great progress during the restoration movement because those men had great respect for God's word. When those men said, "We speak where the Bible speaks," they meant that they had respect for the word of God. It is true that those men did not know much about methods but they knew a lot about the message. They may not have known much about promotion but they knew the art of preaching. We are hearing much about methods but we must remember that there must be a message with methods. Promotion of the Lord's work is a wonderful thing but we must remember unless there is sound preaching with the promotion our efforts are futile.

WE MUST REEMPHASIZE THE
NEED OF RIGHTEOUS ZEAL

During the days of Alexander Campbell, Barton W. Stone, Walter Scott, Moses E. Lard, Raccoon John Smith, Samuel Rogers and a great host of others, the preaching of the gospel was not an easy life. Those men faced trials, endured heartaches, suffered sickness, disease and many times persecution, yet they faithfully proclaimed God's truth. Why? Because they had a burning zeal for God and it was according to righteousness.

We need in the church today Christian zeal that will lead us to do greater things for God; Christian zeal that will cause us to seize opportunities to gather the fields that are white unto harvest. Rightous zeal is a powerful thing. This zeal motivated Joshua to command the sun to stand still. It was rightous zeal that motivated Jesus to cleanse the temple. Zeal has the voice of thunder, its deeds are like lightning and its words like a two-edged sword.

It is an easy thing for a church to drift into indifference like the church in Laodicea. This church was not disturbed by heresies, or broken up by persecution. Its members were in comfortable circumstances. The services could be maintained without strain; there was no one of a contentious disposition to disturb the peace, so they had drifted into an easygoing way and satisfied themselves with simply keeping things up to a fair average level.

The lukewarm are neither earnest for God, nor utterly indifferent to religion. They are perhaps best described as those who take an interest in religion, but worship of their idol of good taste or good form, leads them to regard enthusiasm as ill-bred and disturbing. This people never put themselves to any inconvenience nor braved any reproach, nor abandoned any comfort, for Christ's sake, but hope to keep well with the world, while flattering themselves that they stand well with God. Carlyle calls this, "The hypocrisy that does not know itself to be hypocritical."

The brethren in Laodicea were not cold, but they were not hot; they were not infidels, but they were not earnest believers; they did not oppose the gospel neither did they defend it; they were not working any mischief, neither were they doing any great good; they were not disreputable in moral character, but they were not distinguished for holiness; they were not irreligious, but they were not enthusiastic in piety.

They had elders and deacons who were excellent pillars of the church if the work of pillars is to sit still and exhibit no motion or emotion. This church, no doubt, had ministers but their wings had been clipped for they did not fly very far in preaching the everlasting gospel. Those ministers in Laodicea may have been shining lights of eloquence, but they were not burning lights of grace setting men's hearts on fire with the gospel.

Our prayer should be, "Oh, God, restore to us that zeal of those restoration preachers and the zeal we had when we first obeyed the gospel."

WE NEED TO REEMPHASIZE THE PREACHING OF THE CROSS

Gal. 6:14, "But God forbid that I should glory, save in the cross of our Lord Jesus Christ, by whom the world is crucified unto me, and I unto the world." The cross meant much to Paul and his contemporaries. It meant much to those restoration preachers. We will not likely appreciate the great truths of God until we have a greater appreciation of Christ and His cross.

Christ and his disciples went to an upper room where he instituted the Lord's Supper. He said to them, "one of you shall betray me." All felt like saying, "it is Judas," but instead said, "Lord is it I?" He then selected three of his disciples and went to the Garden of Gethsemane where he often went to pray. He requested these three disciples to watch with him, and he said, "My soul is exceeding sorrowful even unto death."

Why so sorrowful? Because the aggregated sins of the unnumbered millions, dead, living and unborn were piled upon His head and heart. He was about to be exposed, unaided and unbefriended, to the vengeance that had waited four thousand years for its original claim. He was about to suffer the most excruciating death ever recorded in human history. He was about to be made the victim of the blackest crime in the annals of perfidy. He was about to pass through a test, upon which the eternal welfare of mankind depended. He was to be forsaken and disowned by many as a miserable imposter.

He goes a little farther and falls upon the ground in grief. Nearby was the city of Jerusalem and one could hear the clamor and shouts of priestly mobs in the stillness of the night. The rising moon looked coldly on, and dropped its chilly beams upon the dewdrops which wept in his flowing locks. He was arrested and led from one mock trial to another. A mob was yelling, "Crucify him, Crucify him." Pilate said, "I have examined him before you, and have found no fault in this man; touching those things whereof ye accuse him, I find no evil in him." "Crucify him, Crucify him," howled the mob. Pilate asked, "What hath he done?" "Crucify him, Crucify him," shouted the beastly mob.

I have often wondered why some follower of Christ did not cry out to God and say, "Jehovah, destroy this nest of rebels. O God, unlock the thunderbolts of Thy power and wipe them from the face of the earth. These people have always opposed Thee. Their fathers and their grandfathers opposed Thee and showed their hatred for Thee by killing Thy prophets and they will continue to mistreat and kill Thy people. Oh God, deliver Him from this death. When Israel was in bondage, they cried, and You heard and delivered them. When the Hebrew children were cast into the fiery furnace You delivered them. When Daniel was in the lion's den You delivered him. Hear me, O God, can you not deliver Him?" But God would say, "If I deliver him the world will be lost forever."

They then crowned Him with thorns, they spat upon Him, they mocked Him, they scourged Him, and led Him away to Calvary. The cross was lying upon the ground. They stretched Him upon it; the weighty hammer drove the nails through His flesh into the wood. The cross was lifted, and dropped into its place and fastened there.

This was about nine o'clock in the morning. At high noon God sent a blanket of darkness over the face of the earth. The sins of mankind from Eden to the judgment were piled around the cross. Angels shaved the darkness with their weeping wings; demons ran and howled. Sinai rocked while continents shook, and penal thunders long shut up tore through the quivering flesh of the suffering Son of God.

It is now three o'clock in the afternoon. An awful shade of anguish passes over the face of the suffering Saviour—"My God, my God! Why hast thou forsaken me?" Angels have forsaken me—not one remaining—the last one flew away at the advance of the guard in the garden; and the last human friend that might be able to assist me is gone, but all this I could endure so long as Thou wast with me—"Why hast Thou forsaken me?" I am friendless and alone among my enemies—the Jews, the power of Rome supported by its conquering legions, and all hell are against me, but oh, "My God, my God," my only Stay, "Why hast Thou forsaken me?" Jesus has undertaken the work of redemption, and has taken the sinner's place, and He must feel God's displeasure. But this is enough—the cup of His suffering is rapidly filling, and now it is mounted full to the brim, and He is dying. Dying now! O God, He is dying! Look at the pale brow, His bloody face, His sinking eyes, His quivering lips. The Lord of Glory is dying! Here it, Jerusalem! Hear it, Patriarchs! Hear it, tombs of the Prophets! Hear it, Angels, and tell it as you fly, till all the stars shall put on mourning and like Rachel of old go down to the judgment weeping for her children.

Jesus bowed His head and gave up the ghost. Earth quaked, her continents reeled, her mountains bowed, Lebanon shook his frosty top and all his cedars groaned, the granite split, the limestone arches of Machpelah's cave rent and shivered, threatened to crush to finer dust the bones of Abraham. The bloody sword of justice has been satisfied, the veil in the temple has been rent from top to bottom. The sinner may now have his sins forgiven. The work is now done and Jesus dropped the keystone in the last and highest arch, and placed a corner stone, the rejected Corner Stone, stained with blood, hewn out of the diamond rocks of heaven upon the summit of the last and highest corner, and said, "It is finished!" This sound was whispered among the rocks and trees until every mountain peak and every island shouted, "It is finished!" These words were shouted into space and also were shouted at the gates of hell. We must remember that Jesus Christ was lifted up on the cross that we might be saved from our sins.

THE CHURCH

This lecture delivered at Lubbock Christian College, 1973.

The church of Christ is a divine institution for the spiritual welfare of mankind. All great enterprises are the result of much planning, thought and sacrifice. The Church of our Lord came into existence through much suffering, sacrifice, and culminating in the tragedy of the cross. The church is not something visionary or unsubstantial, but a real government, exercising its authority over men in the spiritual realm.

The church existed in the purpose of God through all ages. We may, therefore, expect that this church which had its existence in the eternal purpose of God would be a subject of prophecy. We read,

> And many nations shall come, and say, Come, and let us go up to the mountain of the Lord, and to the house of the God of Jacob, and he will teach us of his ways, and we will walk in his paths: for the law shall go forth out of Zion, and the word of the Lord from Jerusalem." (Micah 4:2). And it shall come to pass in the last days, that the mountain of the Lord's house shall be established in the top of the mountains, and shall be exalted above the hills: and all nations shall flow unto it. And many people shall go and say, Come ye and let us go up to the mountain of the Lord, to the house of the God of Jacob; and he will teach us of his ways, and we will walk in his paths: for out of Zion shall go forth the law, and the word of the Lord from Jerusalem. (Isa. 2:2-3).

This church was set up, firmly fixed and organized on the first Pentecost after the resurrection of Jesus Christ from the dead. The prophetic utterance had been fulfilled, the human cry for mercy had been heard and answered and about three thousand souls became members of this church that the prophets of God had been talking about for hundreds of years.

I am talking about the church that Jesus built.

> When Jesus came into the coasts of Caesarea Philippi, he asked his disciples, saying, Whom do men say that I the Son of man am? And they said, Some say that thou art John the Baptist: some, Elias; and others, Jeremias, or one of the prophets. He saith unto them, But whom say ye that I am? And Simon Peter answered and said, Thou art the Christ, the Son of the living God. And Jesus answered and said unto

him, Blessed art thou, Simon Barjona: for flesh and blood hath not revealed it unto thee, but my Father which is in heaven. And I say also unto thee, That thou art Peter, and upon this rock I will build my church; and the gates of hell shall not prevail against it. And I will give unto thee the keys of the kingdom of heaven: and whatsoever thou shalt bind on earth shall be bound in heaven: and whatsoever thou shalt loose on earth shall be loosed in heaven. (Matt. 16:13-19).

I am speaking of the church that includes all who have believed on Christ, repented of their sins and have been baptized, upon a confession of their faith, for the remission of sins. This is the body of Christ, the flock of Christ; the household of faith, the family of God, the church of the first born, whose names are written in heaven; the church that has one great head, one shepherd, one chief bishop, and that is Jesus Christ.

The church of our Lord is truly Catholic. It is not the church of any one nation or people; its members are to be found in every part of the world where the gospel is preached and obeyed. In the church where there is no difference between Jew and Greek, black and white, bond nor free but all are one in Christ Jesus.

This church will truly be glorious at the end. When all earthly glory is passed away then shall this church be presented without spot before God the father's throne. Thrones, principalities, and powers upon earth shall come to nothing but the church of the first born shall shine as the stars at the last day, and be presented with joy before the Father's throne, in the day of Christ's appearing. When the Lord's jewels are made up, and the manifestation of God takes place, one church only will be named, and that is the church of our Lord Jesus Christ. Unless one belongs to the church of our Lord, he is nothing but a lost soul. He may have great privileges; he may enjoy great wealth, knowledge and social standing but unless he belongs to the body of Christ he is lost.

THE ONE TRUE CHURCH

The church of our Lord was organized in the city of Jerusalem, on the first Pentecost after the resurrection of Jesus from the dead. It is interesting to note that all the forms of speech used referring to the church are singular in number; thus, "Kingdom of Heaven," "Kingdom of God," "Household of faith," "House of God," "The pillar and ground of the truth," "The body," "Temple of God." Where the word 'churches' occurs in the plural number it has reference to the congregations worshipping at particular places, and not to the Kingdom, body or church as a whole.

Paul tells the Ephesian brethren that there is one body.

> Endeavouring to keep the unity of the Spirit in the bond of peace. There is one body, and one Spirit, even as ye are called in one hope of your calling; One Lord, one faith, one baptism, One God and Father of all who is above all, and through all, and in you all. (Eph. 4:3-6). For as we have many members in one body, and all members have not the same office: So we, being many, are one body in Christ, and every one members one of another. (Rom. 12:4-5).

These verses clearly teach that Christ has but one organized body upon this earth.

This church is built upon Christ, and not upon some man, or creed or dogma of man. "For other foundation can no man lay than that is laid, which is Jesus Christ." (I Cor. 3:11). Any church built upon some man is a human church and has no right to exist. Every saved person is a member of the church over which Christ is reigning today. One does not have a choice in becoming a member of the Lord's church, for when he obeys the gospel he is born into God's family. He does not select the church of which he will become a member. God adds to the church all that obey him. May I emphasize the fact, that the only way to get into the church of our Lord is to obey the gospel and become such as should be saved, and the Lord will add you to it. "Praising God, and having favour with all the people. And the Lord added to the church daily such as should be saved." (Acts 2:47).

The church was brought into existence in order to make known to all the universe the perfections of God; to set forth to all rational beings God's true character; to make known to every transgressor that there is a place of refuge. "To the intent that now unto the principalities and powers in heavenly places might be known by the church the manifold wisdom of God." (Eph. 3:10). The plan of redemption is far-reaching in its influence and effect. The mission of the church embraces the whole world. It's mission is to save the sinners, to bring back those who have drifted away, to rescue the fallen, to strengthen the faith, love and devotion of all of God's family.

When we look about us today and see the terrible inroads that sin is making in our nation, in our homes, and in many local congregations of God's people, we should be aroused from our lethargy and begin at once to be more concerned about driving sin from our nation and from the church of the Lord Jesus Christ. It is our duty as members of the church to conserve and keep pure the truth that God has revealed by his Spirit, and to proclaim this truth throughout the world. "Beloved, when I gave all diligence to write unto you of the common salvation, it was needful for me to write unto you, and exhort you that ye should earnestly contend for the faith which was once delivered unto the saints." (Jude 3). Just as water is purified by its own activity, so the church is kept pure by its activity. There is not anything that will drive out sin, division and confusion from the church as will activity. A stagnated church becomes a breeding place for sin, division and every kind of evil work.

Many institutions are established for the select few; others are nation wide, but the church of our Lord makes a universal appeal. In the great commission, Jesus told his disciples to go into all the world. "And he said unto them, Go ye into all the world, and preach the gospel to every creature." (Mk. 16:15). Every creature was a subject to whom this message was to be delivered. Christ said, "Come unto me, all ye that labour and are heavy laden, and I will give you rest. Take my yoke upon you, and learn of me; for I am meek and lowly in heart; and ye shall find rest unto your souls. For my yoke is easy, and my burden is light." (Matt. 11:28-30). Even if one is steeped in sin, hope is still held out. Even if we have forsaken our Lord and been a backslider, still Christ stands at the portals of heaven and beckons us back to him. The church was established for the wise and for the ignorant; for the high and for the low; it was for the wise and the simple; it was for the old age and the young. It includes all the saved of the world.

THE ORGANIZATION OF THE CHURCH IS PERFECT
BUT THE MEMBERS ARE IMPERFECT.

If God had not revealed to us the imperfections of the members of those congregations of the first century we would become discouraged and would give up and fall by the wayside. If God had only revealed the virtues and admirable traits of the early church Christianity would be a discouraging thing for all of God's people.

Let us take a look at the church at Corinth. They were divided over preachers. Some among them said they were of Paul, others were of Apollos, some were of Peter and we are told some were of Christ.

Now I beseech you, brethren, by the name of our Lord Jesus Christ, that ye all speak the same thing, and that there is no divisions among you; but that ye be perfectly joined together in the same judgment. For it hath been declared unto me of you, my brethren, by them which are of the house of Chloe, that there are contentions among you. Now this I say, that every one of you saith, I am of Paul; and I of Apollos, and I of Cephas; and I of Christ. Is Christ divided? was Paul crucified for you? or were ye baptized in the name of Paul? (I Cor. 1:10-13).

Paul said the brethren at Corinth were carnal.

And I brethren, could not speak unto you as unto spiritual, but as unto carnal, even as unto babes in Christ. I have fed you with milk, and not with meat: for hitherto ye were not able to bear it, neither yet now are ye able. For ye are yet carnal: for whereas there is among you envying, and strife, and divisions, are ye not carnal, and walk as men? (I Cor. 3:1-3).

In the fifth chapter of I Cor. Paul said that some of the brethren in the church at Corinth had committed such sins that had not even been named among the Gentiles. They had in their midst a low, degraded man who was living with his father's wife. Many of them seem to be puffed up instead of mourning over this sinful condition. Paul rebuked them sharply and told them such an individual should be delivered to satan.

We read in I Corinthians the sixth chapter that some of the members of the Corinthian church were going to law one with another. "I speak to your shame. Is it so, that there is not a wise man among you? No, not one that shall be able to judge between his brethren? But brother goeth to law with brother, and that before the unbelievers." (I Cor. 6:5-6). Paul rebukes them by saying; "Know ye not that the unrightous shall not inherit the Kingdom of God." In I Corinthians the eleventh chapter we read how the church at Corinth had desecrated the worship of God by turning the Lord's supper into a pagan feast. Paul condemned them for this sin by saying.

When ye come together therefore into one place, this is not to eat the Lord's supper. For in eating every one taketh before other his own supper: and one is hungry, and another is drunken. What? have ye not houses to eat and to drink in? or despise ye the church of God, and shame them that have not? What shall I say to you? shall I praise you in this? I praise you not. (I Cor. 11:20-22).

In the fifteenth chapter of I Corinthians we read about some who had even denied the resurrection of the dead. These teachers were creating dissension and subverting the very foundation of the faith. For if there is no resurrection, then Christ is not risen, and if Christ is not risen, there is no resurrection and they are of all men most miserable.

I am not thankful that these conditions existed in the church at Corinth. But I am thankful, since they did exist, that God has recorded them that we may read and take courage. If God had never recorded any sin of the early congregations, if all these ugly things had been left out of the letters that Paul wrote to the churches, and only made references to absolute purity and perfection, love and harmony, peace and prosperity, we, no doubt, would become discouraged and give up.

It is interesting to observe how Paul addressed this church. I am sure that some of my self-righteous brethren would not have addressed this church as did the apostle Paul. Some of my brethren would not have attended a gospel meeting over in Corinth, and the thought of working with the church at Corinth, to many preachers of this twentieth century, would be ridiculous. It would be interesting to hear one of our modern preachers, who had just spent twelve months with the church at Corinth, and looking for a place to move, talking to his preaching brethren at a preacher's luncheon about the church at Corinth. No doubt, this preacher would say, "I cannot recommend this church to any one, etc." Brother, would you have announced a gospel meeting at Corinth, if you had lived at that time?

Now, I want you to listen to the apostle Paul as he addresses the church at Corinth.

Unto the church of God which is at Corinth, to them that are sanctified in Christ Jesus, called to be saints, with all that in every place call upon the name of Jesus Christ our Lord, both their's and our's. Grace be unto you, and peace, from God our Father, and from the Lord Jesus Christ. I thank my God always on your behalf, for the grace of God which is given you by Jesus Christ; That in every thing ye are enriched by him, in all utterance, and in all knowledge. Even as the testimony of Christ was confirmed in you: So that ye come behind in no gift; waiting for the coming of our Lord Jesus Christ: Who shall also confirm you unto the end, that ye may be blameless in the day of our Lord Jesus Christ. God is faithful, by whom ye were called unto the fellowship of his Son Jesus Christ our Lord. (I Cor. 1:2-9).

Paul does not apologize for their sins, nor make excuses for their disorders; he encourages the faithful to labor for purity, love and harmony, realizing that they can never bring the church to a perfect state. When we read about these conditions that existed in the church at Corinth, we need not become discouraged, despondent, or cast down when we encounter similar things in our experiences.

What would you do if you had belonged to a congregation like the one in Corinth? Would you stay and try to correct these matters or would you do as many of our brethren do in this age, ask for a letter of recommendation that you might worship in another congregation. We need much teaching in the church about members running from congregation to congregation because they do not approve of what is going on in the church where they are worshipping. If one does not have faith in the brethren where he is worshipping, he ought not ask them to give him a letter of recommendation when he leaves. How can one ask those in whom he has not confidence to give him a letter of recommendation?

ALL SPIRITUAL BLESSINGS ARE
IN THIS CHURCH

1. All spiritual blessings are in this church. "Blessed be the God and Father of our Lord Jesus Christ, who hath blessed us with all spiritual blessings in heavenly places in Christ." (Eph. 1:3).
2. One becomes a new creature in the church. "Therefore if any man be in Christ, he is a new creature; old things are passed away; behold, all things are become new." (II Cor. 5:17).
3. No condemnation in Christ. "There is therefore now no condemnation to them which are in Christ Jesus, who walk not after the flesh, but after the Spirit." (Rom. 8:1).
4. Salvation is in Christ. "Therefore I endure all things for the elect's sakes, that they may also obtain the salvation which is in Christ Jesus with eternal glory." (II Tim. 2:10).
5. Blessed are the dead that die in the Lord.

> And I heard a voice from heaven saying unto me, Write, Blessed are they which die in the Lord from henceforth: Yea, saith the Spirit, that they may rest from their labours; and their works do follow them. (Rev. 14:13). For above all principality and power, and might, and dominion, and every name that is named, not only in this world, but also in that which is to come: And hath put all things under his feet, and gave him to be the head over all things to the church, Which is his body, the fulness of him that filleth all in all. (Eph. 1:21-23).

Since the church is the fulness of Christ, one cannot have anything in Christ out of the church, then the church would lack that much being the fulness of Christ. But Paul said the church is the fulness of Christ. To be in Christ is to be in the church. If one is in Christ, he is in the church, if he is not in the church, he is not in Christ. If one belongs to Christ, he belongs to the church, if he does not belong to the church, he does not belong to Christ. If you preach Christ, you preach the church. If you preach the church you preach Christ.

Notice how Paul referred to those people before they became members of the church. He said, you were aliens. You were strangers, you were foreigners. You were without God. You were in the world. Every responsible man outside of the church today is still an alien, a stranger, a foreigner without Christ and without hope. But in Christ there is reconcilliation, citizenship and sancitifcation.

IN GOVERNMENT THE CHURCH
IS BOTH AN ABSOLUTE
MONARCHY AND A DEMOCRACY

The church is an absolute monarchy in that Christ is its head.

And he is the head of the body, the church: who is the beginning, the firstborn from the dead; that in all things he might have the preeminence. (Col. 1:18). For the husband is the head of the wife, even as Christ is the head of the church: and he is the saviour of the body. (Eph. 5:23).

Whatever he commands must be obeyed implicitly by the members of the body. The members have no choice in such matters for they belong to Christ. Whatever the Lord commands must not be tampered with by any one. The Lord has spoken concerning faith, man must not change this commandment. The Lord has commanded repentance and we dare not change it. The Lord has spoken concerning confession and we must leave it like it is in the book. The Lord has commanded baptism and we dare not change it or refuse to obey this command. To refuse to obey any of these commands, no matter how honest one is, is to disobey the Lord.

I have the right to do as I please with those things that belong to me, but I do not have the right to do as I please with things that belong to someone else. Baptism, for instance, does not belong to me, it belongs to the Lord; and I must do as he has commanded. The church is not only an absolute monarchy, but it is also a democracy. This is seemingly paradoxical but it is true. The Lord left some things to the common sense of man. Concerning those things that are not essential to man's salvation, the members do have a voice; and may by majority vote decide what they want to do. The Lord said nothing about how many gospel meetings a church is to have per year; the members may decide on this matter. The Lord did not tell us what time of the day we are to meet to eat the Lord's Supper. As long as we meet on the Lord's day, man is free to decide the time of day for himself. The members of the Lord's church may decide for themselves if they want to meet in a rented hall, construct their own building, employ a full time preacher, have two elders or ten elders, have one class or twenty classes. We need to recognize the fact that in doctrinal matters or in essentials the church is an absolute monarchy. In matters of judgment the church is a democracy. We need to keep clear in our minds the difference in essentials and non-essentials in doing the work of the Lord.

THE CHURCH IS THE MOST GLORIOUS INSTITUTION IN THE WORLD BECAUSE CHRIST IS THE HEAD OF IT

Jesus, the founder of the church, was taken down from the cross a bloody corpse and carried away to the grave. On this day hell shouted for joy, death waved her black banner in triumph, sighs ran along amid the bones of the patriarchs and wails of woe were heard throughout the world. But on the third day our Lord came forth from the hadean world more powerful than Samson when he carried away the gates of Gaza.

Marching in his greatness to save, Christ proclaimed liberty to a captive world by saying, "I am he who was dead and I am alive forever more and have in my hands the keys of death, hell and the grave." Oh, thanks be to God, our Lord reigns more gloriously than did Caesar or Napolean. Millions of subjects bow the knee before him and submit to his way. He rules from shore to shore and from zone to zone. His dominion will be as lasting as the beautitudes of the Sermon on the Mount, and cannot perish until truth and love shall die.

WHAT IS YOUR LIFE?

(James 4:13-14)

This lecture delivered to the Graduating Class, 1971 at Alabama Christian College.

WHAT IS YOUR LIFE?

Scientists are diligently at work today studying the mind and body of man in an attempt to discover the secret of life, and the full nature of life is still a great mystery to which God alone has the key to understanding. Therefore, we in an over-simplified manner define life as the time between birth and death. It is the series of experiences in the existence of a human being and the existence is a very short interval of time. James says it is even as a vapour that appeareth for a little while and then vanisheth away.

What person is there among us who has not seen, on numerous occasions, the vapour of steam rising from a boiling pot of water only to be seen for a second or two and then disappear? Well, this is truly characteristic of the brevity of our lives, and the older one gets the more apparent this truth becomes. Therefore, since we live but once in this world, and since life is so short, it becomes very precious.

Benjamin asked, "Dost thou love life?" This is a good question which deserves a frank answer, dost thou love life? I am sure you do. The very first law of nature is the law of self-preservation. Eddie Rickenbacker was, during World War II, given a worldwide mission to inspect U. S. Combat Groups. On October 21, 1942, he left his base in Hawaii in a Flying Fortress to make an 1800 mile trip to Island no. 10. For some unknown reason the pilot was not able to find the island and to conserve fuel and to extend time those on board dropped all high priority mail, official government document, and many personal valuables into the blue Pacific. After having survived this experience by being rescued after twenty-one days in a life raft, he wrote, "Let the moment come when nothing is left but life and you will find that you do not hesitate over the fate of material possessions however deeply they may have been cherished." Paul gave this same advice long before Rickenbacker, "Let us lay aside every weight and the sin which doth so easily beset us and let us run with patience the race that is set before us." Yes, life is precious and should be loved and enjoyed by all.

But many people have already ruined their lives. They have drifted aimlessly along, squandering their time; neglecting their talents;

suppressing wholesome ambitions and sidestepping opportunities until life has no true meaning to them. They are now what they shall be years from now, and all probability are now what they shall be when they leave this world. The world would be just as well off if they had never lived. But you are young and can determine for yourself the kind of life that you desire to live. You, and you alone, must decide this. I want to suggest to you several things that are absolutely necessary if you are to succeed in this life and also in the one to come.

YOU MUST NOW SET YOUR GOAL
Phil. 3:14.

You must decide now if you want to be a doctor, lawyer, engineer, or gospel preacher. To fail to be able to make up your mind is to be a failure.

"Half the wrecks upon life's ocean
If some star had been their guide,
Would have safely reached the harbor
But instead drifted with the tide."

On the walls of a large university is written: "On the plains of hesitation lie the blackened bones of countless millions, who, at the dawn of victory, sat down to rest, and resting, died."

Too many go through life without chart or compass; with little knowledge of where they have been, not much more of where they are and little concern about where they are going. Isaac Errett wrote in the early Twentieth Century, "The great reason that so many fail is that the majority of graduates have no fixed principles—no definite purpose in life." To succeed in life, you cannot be satisfied with mediocrity but must strive for excellence. You must set your goal for eternity. There is not anything that should challenge your attention more than the word, "eternity." Eternity is where God lives on, the righteous shout on, and the damned groan on. Eternity is as high, wide, and grand as God. Eternity is beginningless and endless, it has no parts, no middle, is forever. If all the mountains of the world were pressing upon your brain, it could not weigh more heavily than the thought of eternity. Eternity began when God began and God has no beginning, eternity will end when God ends and God has no ending. You have two alternatives concerning eternity—heaven or hell. It is very important you set your goal for eternity in heaven now, Jn. 14:1-4; II Pet. 1:10; without Christ your life will be a failure.

I STRONGLY RECOMMEND THAT YOU FACE
THE REALITIES OF LIFE

Don't try to alibi your way through life. An alibi is an anesthetic that a coward administers to himself in the presence of painful or difficult duty. The world is full of subjunctive heroes, men and women who ought, would, or should be something, but have been torpedoed by their own alibis.

Youth never contracts a more dangerous habit than that of excusing himself in the presence of difficulty. Worse than the drug habit is the alibi habit. Drugs destroy the body, but an alibi addict is suffering from cancer of the soul. The alibi shooter can find one hundred good reasons why failure is honorable but remains blind to the fact that victory is possible. If the deadly alibi virus gets into a man's moral system, then ambition, initiative, originality, enterprise, and hope die out of the soul.

In the matter of making alibis, putting the blame on others, passing the blame—there is universal guilt. The use of the alibi is as old as Adam, Eve, Aaron, and King Saul. Alibis began in the Garden of Eden, and continue until this day. It is an old game, a wicked game, a cowardly game; the abominable act of dodging responsibility is a wellknown indoor and outdoor sport. Think of Adam, the Federal head of the family race, who found fault with God for giving him Eve. Think of Eve, the first woman, the first wife, the first transgressor, the first mother, preferring the power of a transient wisdom to the power of an abiding love, coveting a trifle and losing a paradise, believing Satan rather than God. She said, "The serpent beguiled me."

Moses—whom God wanted to send to Pharaoh of Egypt—made an argumentative alibi, "O my Lord, I am not eloquent, neither heretofore, nor since thou has spoken unto thy servant, but I am slow of speech, and slow of tongue." (Ex. 4:10). Think of Aaron who said, "The people were set on mischief." Think of Gideon. He fought long and gloriously for Israel, yet when God wanted him to lead the Hebrew armies he offered the alibi of poverty and low social standing . . . . saying: "My family is poor . . . and I am the least in my father's house." King Saul stood head and shoulders above his countrymen. Every inch a man, tall, handsome, and strong. He alibied saying: "The people spared them." Think of Naaman; he ranked high in the court of Syria, but made an angry alibi . . . saying the rivers of Damascus were better than all the waters of Jordan. Think of Jeremiah, that mystic man of God who was as colorful as Joseph's coat, sad as Hosea, brave as Jesus on the cross. When God spoke of his ordination as a prophet he said, "I cannot speak, I am a child." The ten spies alibied by saying, "We are as grasshoppers in their sight." We can see from days of Adam until this day, man has offered alibis for his shortcomings and failures. The most common alibi offered by young people for not assuming the responsibilities of life is: "I am too young."

1. Alexander the Great ascended the throne at twenty, conquered the known world at thirty-three.
2. Julius Caesar captured eight hundred cities and conquered three hundred nations and became a great statesman at an early age.
3. George Washington was appointed a general at nineteen.
4. Lafayette was made general of the whole French army at twenty.
5. Robert Peel was in Parliament at twenty-one.
6. Gladstone was in Parliament before he was twenty-two.
7. Elizabeth Barrett was proficient in Greek and Latin at twelve.
8. Logic flowed from the pen of DeQuincy at twelve.
9. Nelson was a lieutenant in the British Navy before he was twenty.
10. Victor Hugo, the great poet, was famous at the age of thirty. (Eccl. 12:1).

A SUCCESSFUL LIFE CONSISTS OF
HARD WORK

Yes, hard work is a prerequisite to success. The only place that success is found before work is in the dictionary. We can readily see from the success of others that there are no short cuts to greatness. Many concert artists practice eight hours a day when on tour. Ty Cobb practiced base running and sliding until his hips were raw and his uniform stained with blood. Winston Churchill prepared each speech with upmost care; someone said, "Sir Winston has spent most of his life working on his impromptu speeches." Christian excellence will be attained only by those few who are willing to work and toil to perform the mission assigned them by Christ.

The world is like a large family and everyone a child with a chore to perform and no one is a privileged guest so that all others would wait upon his needs. The person who gets ahead in this world is the one who works those extra hours to please his employer. We are living in an age when many want $3.00 for doing $2.00 worth of work. This person will never be a success in life. Those things that come to you without hard work are never appreciated. The world does not owe you anything but you have a tremendous debt to pay to the world. You have a great debt to pay to your parents, your teachers who have worked with you for many years, and to your country which gives you the freedom to choose your own vocation in life.

NEVER BE CONTENT TO BE
JUST AS GOOD

To live a successful life, you must never be content to be just as good as the next man in life. Paul said, "They that measure themselves by themselves are not wise." The story is told of a man who owned a jewelry store. He noticed every day, early in the morning, that a particular gentleman stopped in front of his store, took something out of his pocket, looked at it, and continued on. Finally, the curiosity of the shopkeeper got the best of him, and he confronted his daily visitor to ask him what he was doing. He replied, "I blow the whistle at the factory down the street, and, therefore, I set my watch every morning by the clock in your window lest I should have the wrong time and blow the whistle at the wrong time." The jeweler replied, "That's strange, I've been regulating the clock in the window by your whistle." The point is, when we measure ourselves by ourselves we are using a very poor standard. Let Christ be your standard and perfect model for an honest evaluation of self. Parallel your life to His.

You must have perseverance to succeed in life. Bob Richards, the former Olympic champion, has remarked that there are 10,000 potentials every year who never make it, become unknown. They do not have three essential ingredients necessary to be a champion: Determination; Conquest of self; and Sacrifice. Or in other words, they are not willing to persevere. The price of success is high and must be paid in painful installments over a lifetime, thus many take the coward's way out and quit. But Jesus said, "No man having put his hand to the plow and looking back is fit for the Kingdom." It is that extra hour of study and training, that extra effort that makes the difference between the excellent and mediocre, the great preacher, and the average preacher, the wise doctor and the unwise doctor, the faithful and the unfaithful.

Numbers 6:24-26: "The Lord make his face shine upon thee, and be gracious unto thee; the Lord lift up his countenance upon thee, and give thee peace."

SOME SURPRISES OF THE PRODIGAL SON

This sermon preached at the Plateau Church of Christ, August, 1969.

I read to you this morning from Luke 15:11-32:

> And he said, There was a man who had two sons; and the younger of them said to his father, Father, give me the share of property that falls to me. And he divided his living between them. Not many days later, the younger son gathered all he had and took his journey into a far country, and there he squandered his property in loose living. And when he had spent everything, a great famine arose in that country, and he began to be in want. So he went and joined himself to one of the citizens of that country, who sent him into his fields to feed swine. And he would gladly have fed on the pods that the swine ate; and no one gave him anything. But when he came to himself he said, How many of my father's hired servants have bread enough and to spare, but I perish here with hunger! I will arise and go to my father, and I will say to him, Father, I have sinned against heaven and before you; I am no longer worthy to be called your son; treat me as one of your hired servants. And he arose and came to his father. But while he was yet at a distance, his father saw him and had compassion, and ran and embraced him and kissed him. And the son said to him, Father, I have sinned against heaven and before you; I am no longer worthy to be called your son. But the father said to his servants, Bring quickly the best robe, and put it on him; and put a ring on his hand, and shoes on his feet; and bring the fatted calf and kill it, and let us eat and make merry; for this my son was dead, and is alive again; he was lost, and is found. And they began to make merry. Now his elder son was in the field; and as he came and drew near to the house, he heard music and dancing. And he called one of the servants and asked what this meant. And he said to him, Your brother has come, and your father has killed the fatted calf, because he has received him safe and sound. And he was angry and refused to go in. His father came out and entreated him, but he answered his father, Lo, these many years I have served you, and I never disobeyed your command; yet you never gave me a kid, that I might make merry with my friends. But when this son of yours came, who has devoured your living with harlots, you killed for him the fatted calf! And he said to him, Son, you are always with me, and all that is mine is yours. It was fitting to make merry and be glad, for this your brother was dead, and is alive; he was lost and is found.

In all probability this is one of the most beautiful readings in the New Testament, yet it is sad in so many ways. It is beautiful because of the attitude of the father toward one who had sinned. It is sad because of the ugly attitude that this elder brother had who claimed to be so righteous. Everything we have in the Bible has been put there for a purpose, and no doubt God has put this in the Bible for us to make application to our own lives.

I want to talk to you about some of the surprises that came in the life of the prodigal son. Someone has said that every individual that goes to heaven will have some surprises when he gets there; one surprise being that some of the very people that he thought would not be there will be some of the first ones he will see. That may be true because of our hazy thinking, perhaps because our hearts are not always pure. For various reasons we may have the wrong thoughts about other people.

Another surprise is that some of the very people that we thought would be there, are not there. But possibly, the greatest surprise of all will be that we made it. Thus, these are some of the surprises, because after all, if we are saved it will be by the mercy of God and his goodness. I want to talk to you for a few minutes about some of the surprises in the life of this prodigal son so that you may apply these six surprises to your own life.

HE WAS SURPRISED THAT HIS FATHER
GAVE HIM HIS PORTION

This son was surprised that the father gave him his portion of the goods. No doubt, this son had thought about leaving home many, many times. I suppose that sometime during the lifetime of every boy comes a thought of leaving home. The prodigal figures "If I should go to my father and talk to him about it he will not give me the portion of goods that belong to me. In other words, when my father dies I will receive certain things, but if I should go to him now, and say, Father, I want these things, I am going to leave home, he would not give them to me." So it may have come as a great surprise to this young man when he went to his father and said, "I want the portion of goods that belong to me, I am not willing to wait until you die," that his father actually granted his request.

He may have reasoned like this: "Now I am a young man. It may be that you will live for years and years, and at the time of your death I may be up in years. Therefore, I would not have time to use this money as I would like to use it. I am young now; I am ambitious; I have great aims; I have great desires; therefore, I want the portion of goods that belong to me **now!**" It must have been a great surprise when his father said, "If that is the way you feel about it, I will give you your portion."

I think the lesson that is taught here is this: whenever we indicate to God That we are going to do certain things and our heart is set on that, there is no doubt in my mind but that God says, "Go to it!" That is what the father said to the prodigal son. I suppose, surely, that the father tried to reason with him, "This is not best, this is really not what you need." But the son said, "I want it! I want it now!" The father said,"That is fine, then take it." That is the reason God leaves some people alone today. I think when a Christian is indifferent and unconcerned about the work of the Lord, about the people lost and dying round about him; when he shows no interest in the work of the church, shows no interest in Bible study, shows no interest in visiting the sick, shows no interest in promoting the Kingdom of God; when he is just one of these traditional church members who comes and eats the Lord's Supper on the first day of the week, then I think God says, "I have given him up!" So, the father gave the prodigal his portion.

HE WAS SURPRISED AT HOW EASILY
HE COULD LEAVE

It must have been a great surprise to learn how easy it was for him to leave home and to go into this far country. You know, it is such an easy thing for an individual to drift away from the faith. We have enough members in the body of Christ today to completely evangelize the world, if all were committed and dedicated to Jesus Christ. But, do you know what happens? So many are like the prodigal son; they drift into a far country from this faithfulness and steadfastness. I am sure that most of you have been out on the water in boats to fish. You have perhaps chosen a particular spot to fish, stopped, and would be fishing, when after a while you observed that you were fifteen or twenty feet from the original spot where you intended to fish, though you were never conscious of the fact that you were drifting.

This is exactly what happens to many people who are members of the body of Christ. They are unconsciously drifting into indifference. I have never in my life known a member of the church to stand up on Lord's Day morning and say, "Brethren, I have an announcement to make. I have been faithful to all the services. I have put the kingdom of God first in my life, and now I want to announce that beginning this evening at six o'clock, I am making other plans. I do not intend to come to the Sunday evening services any longer. Now, you know I have been attending Wednesday night Bible study for years, very faithfully; every time you have come you have seen me there. I am announcing that I am through with this, beginning next Wednesday night! You also know I have been known in this congregation as one who would visit the sick, but I am telling you, I am not going to visit another room in the hospital. I am through!" Have you ever heard a person make an announcement like that in church? Have you? Yet, all over this country, in every congregation we have dozens and dozens, and in some places hundreds of members just like this. They do not go on Sunday night; they do not go on Wednesday night; they do not visit the sick; they do not work. Well, someone asks, "How in the world did he ever get like that?" Just like the prodigal son got into the far country. After he got there, he probably looked back and said, "You know, I never realized it was such an easy thing."

Brother, one of the easiest things on God's earth to do is to drift away from faithfulness. It is the easiest thing! You do not have to exert any energy, you do not have to pray, and you do not even have to think. Just think about that now! You do not even have to think. Now, that is the reason that we have people who move into parts of the country like this and never darken the doors of a building; they do not think nor care. That is why some people who come on Lord's Day morning, eat the Lord's Supper, then forget all about righteousness until next Lord's Day morning. They may not get the surprise in this life, but after they die, they are going go get a shocking surprise.

The sad thing is this, the prodigal son never did come to his senses until he had sunk just about as deep in sin as a man could sink. All indications are that it never dawned on him that he was drifting away from his home, his father, and into sin. This is the way people drift away from the church and from God today. The father in this parable represents God, and this prodigal son represents the Christian. The parable shows how a man can drift away from the church.

You possibly have people in this community who are just traditional church members. How much do they do to promote the Kingdom of God? "Well," you say, "they come and eat the Lord's Supper." Maybe it will help you to understand the lesson better if I ask you to do this in your mind. Do not take out a pencil and paper, unless you just want to, but in your mind, write this down: "On Sunday morning I go to worship, I eat the Lord's Supper, I go home." Now, write down what else you do. Just take the Sunday morning service out of your spiritual life, and I ask you, what else are you doing? That will give you some idea how you stand spiritually.

I have talked to members of the church who have told me, "Now Brother Black, I never realized, I never dreamed I would drift to this place in life, but I was here before I knew it." This is exactly what happens to the spiritual life of many people. They are never conscious of drifting. For this reason Paul said, "We ought to give the more earnest heed to the things that we have heard lest at any time we should let them slip, or lest at any time we drift."

Why feedest thou on husks so coarse and rude?
I could not be content with angel's food.

How camest thou companion to the swine?
I loathed the courts of heaven, the choir divine.

Who bade thee crouch in hovel dark and drear?
I left a palace wide to hide me here.

Harsh tyrant's slave who made thee, once so free?
A father's rule too heavy seemed to me.

What sordid rags float round thee on the breeze?
I laid immortal robes aside for these.

An exile through the world who bade thee roam?
None, but I wearied of a happy home.

Why must thou dweller in a desert be?
A garden seemed not fair enough to me.

Why sue a beggar at the mean world's door?
To live on God's large bounty seemed so poor.

What has thy forehead so to earthward brought?
To lift it higher than the stars I thought.

Anonymous

HE WAS SURPRISED AT DEPTH OF SIN

The prodigal was surprised at the depth to which one could sink in sin. No doubt, when he left home, his aim, his ambition, and his desire at this time was to do something great in this world. In all probability the father tried to talk him out of it, but the chances are that the father still said in his heart, "This boy is a bright young man and will be a success in life. He may not be doing the wise thing now, but some day you will hear from him. He will be a leader of men, because he has the makings of a man in him."

We are told that this young man went away from home, and spent his money in riotous living. While he was spending his money, oh, the friends were many, but after awhile he realized that he was in the depth of sin. He realized that it was such a difficult thing for him to pull out of it. I am sure that if you had told him when he left home, "You are not doing the wise thing, and one of these days you will go so far into sin that even you will be shocked," he likely would have doubted that.

I remember there was a man in the Plateau congregation who obeyed the gospel immediately after the first sermon he heard. This was when we were in our first new building about twenty-two or three years ago. I shall never forget how faithful this person was, attending every service. Later we built a minister's home, on which he also worked. He would work on his job all day, then he would work all afternoon and into the hours of the night on this building. Three or four years went by, and he took an additional job. Soon I observed that he was missing services on Wednesday evening, and it was not long until he started missing services on Sunday evening. I went to him and reminded him that he was not as faithful as he once had been, and admonished him to be careful. I could detect that he was drifting, even though he was not conscious of it. Then it was not long until occasionally he would miss Lord's Day morning. Again I went to his house to have a talk with him. We talked for a long time, and he said, "Brother Black, I would never drift away from the church." Of course, I knew he was drifting then, but he was not conscious of it. He seemed to think he was just as faithful as he had ever been. Oh, he admitted that sometimes he could not come because he was letting other things hinder him. So, several months went by, and then a year or two, and I have an idea it has been fifteen years since that man has darkened the door of the house of God. They tell me now that he drinks, he curses, he carouses, he is rearing his children outside the church, he has had family trouble; all of these things because he started drifting. He was once such a good man, such a faithful man, but never able to realize that he was drifting. You could never have made him believe that he would sink this deep into sin.

I am sure the prodigal son never thought he would sink so deep in sin, either. Would it not be a wonderful thing if we could impress upon the minds of people who are members of the church when they begin to slip, and to drift a little, that one day they will wind up in the depths of sin. "You may loose your home, you may loose your children." But the sad thing is that, like the prodigal son, one never realizes it until he is already in the depths of sin. Then he will ask, "How could one sink so low?"

HE WAS SURPRISED THAT NO MAN GAVE TO HIM

The prodigal was surprised that "no man gave to him" in his hour of deep need while dwelling in sin-land. Oh, what a shock this must have been! No doubt, he cried out, "Where are my friends?" I remember that when I had all this money I could not push them back. I remember that everywhere I went people gathered round me, and talked about what a wonderful, jolly person I was. But now all my money is gone; I am in the depths of sin; I am helpless, hungry, and nearly naked. "Where are all of my friends?" Oh, what a surprise it was when no man would give to him.

Once an individual told me about his brother who had drifted away from Christ, and had gotten in with a group of hoodlums—wild people. They were operating as gangsters, hauling whiskey into counties and states where it was prohibited by law. He told how his brother had often boasted of the closeness of these friends of his, and how he had learned out here in this world that these were real men, men who would stick by you. They were friends. Later this brother was arrested and thrown in jail. While he was in jail, waiting to be tried and eventually sentenced to the penitentiary, these "dear friends" took his clothes, even his shoes, and his shirts; they sold them and used the money for themselves. That is the friendship of the world!

Oh, while this prodigal son had his money, he had plenty of friends but when he had spent all of his money, and was not living in sin, he learned he had no real friends. What a shock this must have been! The Bible says that no man would give to him, so he hired himself to a citizen who sent him out into the field to feed swine.

Now, this boy was a Jew. There was not anything more detestable to a Jew than swine, or hogs. But when he employed himself to this citizen, he was sent down to the hog pen to tend the hogs. That is how low he had sunk into sin. That is what sin will do to you, too. That is what sin has already done to this nation. While he was feeding the swine, the Bible says, "He would have fain filled his belly with the husks that the swine did eat, but no man would give to him." Thus he decided to repent and to go back to his father.

HE WAS SURPRISED THAT HE COULD REPENT

Oh, how many times have I talked to individuals who talk like this, "Well, I tell you, Brother Black, I have lived in sin so long and I have lived such a wicked life, that I do not believe I can repent." The devil can convince an individual that he cannot even repent of his sin.

I remember preaching in a meeting where I talked to an elderly gentleman about obeying the gospel. He told me, "Brother Black, I have lived in sin so long; I have lived in sin ever since I reached the age of accountability, I am so hardened to righteousness and goodness that I do not believe I could repent." I tried to reason with him that he could; but he is dead now, and he never obeyed the gospel. He never did repent. Sin had made him believe that he could not repent.

No doubt, if someone had gone to this prodigal son while he was spending his money in riotous living, it would have been difficult to make him believe that he could repent. If someone had reasoned, "Son, you better come to your senses, because this sin is going to wreck your life," he likely would have said, "You know, I have lived in sin so long I cannot repent. I have gone so far from home, I cannot repent." But when he got hungry down in the hog pen feeding those swine, and no man would give to him, he said to himself, "I would gladly fill my belly with the husks that the swine did eat." It was then that he came to himself.

You know it is a very unfortunate thing that often some calamity has to happen to an individual to bring him to his senses. This is not always true, but many times it is a terrible calamity that brings a man to his senses. Is it not awful that man will become so hardened and rebellious toward God that he will not come back to God until some terrible calamity happens? When the calamity came, however, the prodigal said, "I will arise and go to my father, and will say unto him, 'Father, I have sinned against heaven, and before thee.' " In essence he was saying, "I have sinned against you; I have sinned against my family. I am not blaming anyone but myself. I am not going to say, ' If I have done anything wrong, forgive me.' " He simply said, "I am going home and say, 'Father, I have sinned.' " You may observe his attitude of complete humility as he says, "Father, I am not worthy to be called your son, but if you will just make me one of the hired servants, I will be pleased and happy."

Does that lamp still burn in my Father's house
Which he kindled the night I went away?
I turned once beneath the cedar boughs,
And marked its gleam with a golden ray;
Did he think to light me home some day?

Hungry here with the crunching swine,
Hungry harvest have I to reap;
In a dream I count my Father's kine,
I hear the tinkling bells of his sheep,
I watch his lambs that browse and leap.

There is plenty of bread at home,
His servants have bread enough and to spare;
The purple wine-fat froths with foam,
Oil and spices make sweet the air
While I perish hungry and bare.

Rich and blessed those servants, rather
Than I who see not my Father's face!
I will arise and go to my Father's—
"Fallen from sonship, beggared of grace,
Grant me, Father, a servant's place."

W. Buxton

He was, no doubt, greatly surprised at the reception he received back home. He wondered, I am sure, if his father would accept him, because he knew he had lived a very wicked life bringing shame and reproach upon his father's name. His brother said he spent his money with harlots; he had lived a terrible life. So it must have been a great surprise, as he drew near his home, to see his father running to meet him. No doubt, the prodigal's guilty conscience had made him reason that the father would be somewhat distant; maybe if I can plead with my father he will forgive me; maybe I can talk him into letting me work for him. But as he nears home he sees his father running toward him. That is the love that God has for every sinner. And even though it may be difficult, it may be strange to us, yet that is the love which God has for every sinner. The only time in the Bible that God is pictured as running is when he is running to meet a sinner; the father running to meet the son.

I remember reading once of a young man who left his home, lived in sin, and he knew that he had brought shame and reproach upon his family name and upon his parents and community. After he had reached the depths of sin and was in trouble, had no money and had become so sorry and so trifling until people would not give him aid, he realized what a terrible mess he had made of his life and wanted to go back home. But, "My," he thought, "what an awful thing that would be to go back home and confess to all these people I have been a failure, and I have made a miserable mess of my life." Have you ever thought about the courage that would take? Then he thought about the embarrasment it would bring to his father, to his people. So one day he sat down and wrote his father a letter. He told his father what a sinful life he had lived; how he had brought shame and reproach upon his name, and he said, "Really, I am not worthy to wear this name any longer, but I want to come back home. You may not want me to come back because of the way I have lived and what I have done to your name. But on a certain day I plan to board the train that passes the old home place. If I am welcome at home, I want you to take a white cloth and hang it on the limb of one of those trees, visible from the track. Then when I pass by if I see that white cloth, I will get off the train; I will know I am welcome; but if I do not see it, I will just keep going because I know I have disgraced you."

So on this day when the boy started home, he was very nervous. A gentleman sitting across the aisle detected his nervousness, and offered help. The young man then told the miserable story of his life, including the letter recently sent to his father. Then he said, "I am just wondering if that white cloth will be hanging on that tree." The gentleman then suggested that he watch for the white flag too, so they would be sure not to miss it. When they came around the curve and the tree was in sight, the gentleman exclaimed, "Young man, there is a white cloth on every limb of that tree!"

Actually, on God's tree of love, there is a white cloth on every limb, saying to the erring child of God, "Come home." Man has never been able to fully comprehend that love. What a surprise the father's love must have been to this prodigal son, who was going home shoeless, unshaven, unshorn, friendless, and almost naked.

I can see this father in my mind as he looks down the road and sees some figure. His first thought, perhaps, is "that boy walks like my son." Then as the figure draws close the father reasons, "No, that is not my son; that is a tramp, a bum; he could not be my son. He is barefoot and almost naked; but there is something in his walk that reminds me of my son." Then as the boy draws near, the father realizes that he is his own son; and the Bible says he runs and he falls upon him. He embraces him; he even kisses him, and says, "Once my son was lost but now he is found; once he was dead and now he is alive." He was thrilled beyond expression. And he said to the servant, "Bring forth the fatted calf. Let us eat and be merry because my son has come home." He even took his ring and he put that upon his fingre. He bought shoes and put on his feet. He took his best robe and said, "Put this on my son." Oh, what a surprise this must have been to this son to know that his father would receive him with such open arms.

HE WAS SURPRISED AT THE ATTITUDE
OF THE OLDER BROTHER

Finally, it must have been a shock and surprise to this prodigal son to observe the ugly attitude of his elder brother. I have often thought to myself, would it not have been wonderful if this parable had stopped here? But actually, all of these things have been said to teach the next point. When the father received him, they began making merry. The older brother, out in the field, heard music, singing, and dancing. Oh, they were so happy! He had never heard such joyful people in his life. I want you to notice his attitude—he would not even go in. He called one of the servants and said, "What are they doing in there?" And the servant thought he should be thrilled to death; "Why," he said, "your brother has come home! Your father is happy—the happiest man I have ever seen in my life because his son has come home. You ought to see the old man. He is thrilled to death!" The elder brother said, "I am not going in. I am not going to have anything to do with him." Is it not awful, that a man's heart can be like that? So the servant went in and told the man of the house that his elder son would not come in.

What a shock that must have been to the father. He goes out and tries to reason with him. The son said, "All these years I have been here with thee, and I have never transgressed your law;" but all the time he was saying, "I have never transgressed your law," he was breaking his father's heart as he said it. This is what self-righteousness will do for a person. No doubt, the father begged, "Come in, your brother has come home," but he would not even call him his brother. He said, "When **this thy son** came home," in otherwords, he is not **my** brother, I am having nothing to do with him. But then, as the father talked to him, he said, "When this **your** brother did come home."

When the parable closes, even though this son had lived a terrible life, even though he had sunk deep in sin, the prodigal son is on the inside with his father's love and fellowship; the elder brother, who was a self-righteous, Pharisaical person, was on the outside, separated from the Father.

This is one of the most beautiful parables in the Bible, and the thing that Jesus was primarily condemning was the ugly Pharisaical attitude which we manifest if we are not careful. When a sinner comes home, someone may say "he is not sincere; he will not hold out; I have seen that before." But that was not the way the loving father reasoned. So these are the surprises in the life of the prodigal son. I am sure these surprises have been experienced, to some degree, in the life of every individual who has been a sinner. But we should rejoice, just as the father did over those who repent of their sins.

This is a wonderful parable. It would mean so much to us in living the Christian life if we would study it, and think about it daily. There are many in this audience, no doubt, like the prodigal son, you need to come home. Will you not step out in the aisle and come while we stand and sing the invitation?

WHAT A LOST SOUL LEARNED IN HELL

This sermon preached in the Gulf Coast Campaign for Christ, Mobile, Alabama in 1965.

The subject that has been announced for tonight is "What a Lost Soul Learned in Hell." I am reading to you from Luke 16:19-31 where it says,

> There was a certain rich man, which was clothed in purple and fine linen, and fared sumptuously, every day: And there was a certain beggar named Lazarus, which was laid at his gate, full of sores, And desiring to be fed with the crumbs which fell from the rich man's table: moreover, the dogs came and licked his sores. And it came to pass, that the beggar died, and was carried by the angels into Abraham's bosom: the rich man also died, and was buried; And in hell he lifted up his eyes, being in torments, and seeth Abraham afar off, and Lazarus in his bosom. And he cried, and said, Father Abraham, have mercy on me, and send Lazarus, that he may dip the tip of his finger in water, and cool my tongue; for I am tormented in this flame. But Abraham said, Son, Remember that thou in thy lifetime receivedst thy good things, and likewise Lazarus evil things: but now he is comforted, and thou art tormented. And besides all this, between us and you there is a great gulf fixed: so that they which would pass from hence to you cannot; neither can they pass to us that would come from thence. Then he said, I pray thee therefore, father, that thou wouldest send him to my father's house: For I have five brethren; that he may testify unto them, lest they also come into this place of torment. Abraham saith unto him, They have Moses and the prophets; let them hear them. And he said, Nay, father Abraham: but if one went unto them from the dead, they will repent. And he said unto him, If they hear not Moses and the prophets, neither will they be persuaded though one rise from the dead.

This is one of the saddest readings in the Bible. It is sad because it talks about a man losing his soul. The word "lost" is one of the saddest words known to man. We sometimes see people who have lost the ability to see. Even though these people may not ask for pity, we do pity them because we know that they cannot behold the beautiful things that God has made. They cannot even look into the face of their beautiful children. They cannot see the trees, the mountains, the rivers, nor the lakes. There are those who have lost their sense of hearing. We pity them because we know that they cannot hear God's people as they join their voices together as we have done on this occasion in singing praises to God. Sometimes we read in the paper that some child has been lost. No one can read something like this without being disturbed, because when we read it the first thing that comes to our mind is the child's wandering around in the forest, running and crying for its mother until finally darkness closes in on it. It runs until it is exhausted, then falls asleep. And we can think of serpents hissing around its body, and owls sitting in the trees hooting above the body. No one can read such without being disturbed. And it is for that reason that people will join hands by the hundreds and go into the forest looking for a little child.

A few years ago, I read a book entitled, **The U. S. Indianapolis**. It was a book written about the terrible tragedy that happened on July 31, 1945. There were 1,196 American boys aboard this ship. It was blown up one minute past midnight on a Sunday night, and a book was written to tell what an awful thing it is to be lost at sea, in water 7,000 feet deep, 250 miles from the closest island with no one in the world knowing where you are. This book told how those boys reacted when they realized they were lost. It tells that when the ship was hit by the enemy, most of those boys got off the ship into the water and spent the night waiting for daylight. They floated on life rafts and pieces of timber and all day Monday they lived in hope because they believed someone would rescue them. Then Monday night came, and during the night they almost froze to death. No one found them. Then Tuesday came. During the day they almost burned to death. By this time they were hungry. They were thirsty. They began to wonder if anyone in the world knew where they were, yet their morale was still high, even on Tuesday. Then Wednesday came; no one had found them. By this time many of those boys had become delirious and hysterical. The book told how those boys reacted when they realized that no one in the world knew where they were. It told how many of the boys went raving mad; how they actually cursed and turned loose and dropped to the bottom of the sea. It told how other boys prayed the most pitiful prayers that ever fell from the lips of mortal man and then would turn loose and fall to the bottom of the sea. And then Thursday came and no one had found them. Thursday night and Friday morning, still no one had found them. It was not until noon on Friday that someone located them. By this time, of the 1,196 boys, only 316 were living. The book impressed one thought upon my mind. It is a terrible thing to be lost.

When I read that book I could not read it without crying because I thought of all those hundreds of boys who went down to the bottom of the sea. But actually there is something a thousand times sadder than that. And that is for a man to lose his soul. And the reason it is so sad for a man to lose his soul is because it is lost for eternity. If an individual just lost his soul for a million years, he would have hope, (think of that, a million years) after he had been in the torments of hell for 500,000 years, then he could say, "It is half over. I just have 500,000 more years to live in this awful torment." After he had lived in hell for 900,000 years then he could say, "I just have another 100,000 years and it will all be over." And beyond any doubt he would look forward to that more than anything else he could imagine. Oh, that would be terrible, but it would not be for eternity. Have you ever seriously thought about being lost for eternity?

He Learned The Meaning of Eternity

This word "eternity" is found only one time in the Bible. Isaiah 57:15:

> For thus saith the high and lofty One that inhabiteth eternity, whose name is Holy; I dwell in the high and holy place, with him also that is of a contrite and humble spirit, to revive the spirit of the humble, and to revive the heart of the contrite ones.

Eternity is that place where God lives on, where the righteous shout on, and where the damned groan on. Eternity is as high, as wide, and as deep as God himself. Eternity is beginningless, it is endless, it has no middle, it has no part. It is just high noon forever and forever. If all the mountains of the world were to press upon one's brain, they could not weigh heavier than the thought of eternity. Eternity always has been and it always will be. You may just as well start out looking for the tomb of God as to look for the end of eternity. You may just as well start out telling someone that you are going to locate the cradle of God as to tell someone that you are going to locate the beginning of eternity. Eternity is forever and forever. It is beginningless, endless, measureless, imperishable, indescribable, and undefinable. Eternity is where the soul will go that is separated from God; the soul of man that is lost. If it were possible for you to mount a chariot drawn by steeds of lightning, and you could travel over rivers, mountains, continents, and seas to the equator and there get your bearings; if you could lash with your whip and drive until those steeds fell, until those axles were ground to dust, and until your bones were lost in some valley where no angels could ever find them, still you could not find the end of eternity.

If you could fly a thousand times faster than the speed of light itself, you could travel for a million years, and you would be no closer to the end of eternity than when you first started. Eternity is like a circle—it has no end. You could circle the earth once, but you would never find the end of eternity. The keys of eternity are tied to the girdle of God, and God with his almighty hands has wound that clock and it will tick and tick and tick forever and forever. And when an individual has lived in eternity for a billion years, he has no less time to live there. Oh eternity, all angels we beg of thee, tell us thy name! The mother of ages, the parent of cycles, that is the place where the soul lives on forever and forever. When we think of being lost and going to this awful place of torment it is almost more than the human mind can comprehend. To those of you who have never rendered obedience to the gospel, and to those of you who are in a lost condition, that is what is waiting for you. And it will just be a few more days until you will lift your eyes up in hell.

Oh, but someone says, "Eternity is time." No, eternity is not time. I can define time. We can break it down in seconds, minutes, hours, days, weeks, months, years, eons; time is only one small segment of eternity! Eternity continues when time ceases. When time ceases, that awful night of eternity will continue for all of those who have disobeyed God. No rational person can think seriously about eternity and then think of rebelling against the law of God.

Now in these verses which we read to you from Luke 16, we read of a man who went to this place we are talking about—hell. He is there not for just a million years, not for a billion years, but he is there for eternity. And, oh, what he would give this night for your opportunity! What he would give this night for your chance! He would say that you have all the hope in the world, and if he could get a message back to you it would be, "Do not sin away the day of grace. Do not spend another day in the kingdom of Satan. Give your life to Jesus Christ. Do that which you know is right." Oh, that is what he would say to you because of the things he learned in hell!

This may seem strange, but there are certain things that God intends for man to learn in life. If he refuses to learn these things here, then God is going to teach them to him in hell. Now, let us observe some of the awful things he learned in the place of torment.

He Learned There Is No Second Chance

No doubt countless millions of people have lived in this world and sinned away the day of grace, hoping, praying, and thinking that there will be another day of grace in this life. But the truth about it is this: when you have heard your last sermon, when you have heard your last invitation in the world, when you have been ushered out into eternity, you will never have another invitation extended to you! You will never hear another gospel sermon that will do you any good. I think the truth about it is that every individual who goes to hell and who has ever heard a gospel sermon will be able to recall every word of that sermon because he will have all eternity to think about it. I think he will recall the preacher's name who preached those sermons. I think he will remember the expression on each preacher's face, because he will have all eternity to think about it. In Hebrews 9:27, the writer says, "For it is appointed unto men once to die and after that the judgment." In John 5:28 Jesus Christ said,

Marvel not at this: for the hour is coming, in which all that are in the graves shall hear his voice, and they shall come forth; they that hath done good, unto the resurrection of life; and they that have done evil unto the resurrection of damnation.

So there is no place to go, my friends, between this life and the next one, to do something about your soul's salvation. When you sin away the day of grace in this life, you are hurled out into eternity to meet God just as you die. There is no second chance after you live your life here. Now you probably have had hundreds of chances and hundreds of opportunities. Some of you have had many opportunities to render obedience to the gospel. You have not done it, but I want you to listen to me. When you finally sin away the day of grace and when you have heard your last sermon and your last invitation in this world, you will go to meet your God unprepared.

It is possible that you may not believe that tonight, because there was a rich man who lived and did not believe it. I do not know how this man reasoned when he heard the prophets preach. I suppose he reasoned like a lot of church members do. They have the thing cut and dried and what the preacher says does not have much bearing on many of them. They are going to live just as they please; and they are going to lift their eyes up in hell, too, just as surely as you live. I have an idea that the rich man folded his hands when he heard those prophets preach, shrugged his shoulders, and said, "I thought the preacher was a little too dramatic tonight. He talked like the world was coming to an end today, and that kind of preaching just does not appeal to me. Well, if I miss it in this life, I will have another opportunity in the next world." But the rich man did not have another opportunity and you are not going to have another opportunity either, when you sin away that day of grace in this life. He learned there is no second chance.

He Learned God Meant What He Said

Now no doubt, of all the things we try to do, one of the most difficult things in the world is to get people to believe that God actually means what he says. If we could convince people that God means what he says, it would not be difficult to get people to render obedience unto the gospel. For instance, suppose an individual wants to know something about faith. We just turn to the Bible, in Hebrews 11:6 and we read, "But without faith it is impossible to please him: for he that cometh to God must believe that he is, and that he is a rewarder of them that diligently seek him." Well, that would forever settle the matter. That is what God said about it. That is not about it; that is it! That is God's truth. I believe what he says.

Next, he says, "I would like to know something about repentance." So we turn to Luke 13:3 and read what the Lord said: "I tell you, Nay: but, except ye repent, ye shall all likewise perish." "Why", the individual says, "I believe that." There would be nothing to argue about if he believed it.

If confession is the topic under discussion, we would merely turn and see what the Lord says about it. In Matthew 10:32 he says, "Whosoever therefore shall confess me before men, him will I confess before my Father which is in heaven." And so that will forever settle the matter concerning the necessity of confessing our faith in Jesus.

Suppose one should say, "I would like to know something about baptism." If he believed that God means what he says, we could follow the same procedure: turn and read. In Mark 16:15-16, he said, "Go ye into all the world, and preach the gospel to every creature. He that believeth, and is baptized, shall be saved; but he that believeth not shall be damned." In Matthew 28:19 the record says, "Go ye therefore, and teach all nations, baptizing them in the name of the Father, and of the Son, and of the Holy Ghost." Somebody says, "I want to argue about that." What do you want to argue about? Do you mean that you do not believe what the Lord said? What would the argument be over? What could we argue about? The Lord said do it! Every infidel knows that the Lord said do it, but the question is, "Do we believe it?" And you know, as well as I, that there are countless thousands of people living that do not believe what the Lord said about it. You have never in your life heard a man say that Jesus did not say it. You have never in your life heard a man say that Jesus did not command it, but you have heard numbers of people say that they do not believe it. It has always been difficult to get people to believe that the Lord means what he says, but I can tell you one thing, my friend: There is a man tonight if he could speak to you he would say, "You had better believe it. You better take the Lord at his word. I lived back there. I know. I did not believe what those prophets said." Every time an invitation is extended and rejected, we cannot keep from asking, "Do they believe what the Lord says?"

He Learned Hell Is Real

Now that, possibly, is more difficult to get over to people than the other things we have mentioned. You know it is interesting to read magazines that tell you what certain ones believe about hell. They read something like this: "We interviewed a certain group of religious teachers. Forty-eight per cent of them say there is no hell; seventy-two per cent say that hell is not real; and sixty-five per cent of a certain group say that hell is not real." I will tell you about one I would like to read. I would like to read where somebody polled the members of the church of Christ, because I would like to know how many among us believe that hell is real. That is one reason why it is so difficult to get people to respond to the gospel; they just do not believe that hell is real. Many convince themselves that hell is some kind of fairy tale, or something that parents tell their children to keep them out of devilment. Every sinner would respond if he believed that hell is real. I am going to convince you that countless numbers of people who are members of the church do not believe that hell is real.

Sometimes in my home congregation the elders will say, "Brother Black, there is a certain individual whom you ought to talk to because he has not been to services in weeks." Have you ever wondered how a conversation goes between the preacher and one of those members? It goes about like this: (knock), he comes to the door. "Brother, we have been missing you at the church services." You would think he would defend himself, but he smiles. He says, "That is right, Brother Black, but let me tell you something so that you will not start preaching to me. I know just as well as you know where I am going. And I know that if I should die in the condition that I am in, I would go to hell." I have often wished that I had courage enough to say to that individual, "You stop mocking God in my presence." Whenever you hear a member of the church talking like that, he is ridiculing God, he is making sport of God and he is mocking God. And there are many members of the church of Christ who mock God every day that they live. You tell me that you believe that there is a burning devil's hell and then you will laugh and joke and talk about it. He talks about going to hell as if he were going to the Gulf, or to the mountains for a vacation, where it is very pleasant. Let me tell you something, my friends, I would be afraid to mock God. I would be afraid to go home and pillow my head, laughing and ridiculing and making sport of God. You tell me that you believe that there is a devil's hell, but you refuse to obey God. You do not believe a word of it!

I am going to convince you that this man is not sincere. Just suppose that after I leave him he has a very pleasant conversation about his trip to hell. He knows where he is going, and seems to be looking forward to it. Faithful Christians and preachers have all heard men talk like that. We have heard about Robert Ingersoll and other infidels and atheists; and we wonder how they can mock God like that.

Once I got a letter from a person down in Florida about our T. V. program. It was the ugliest thing you have ever read in your life. He said every mean, ugly, hateful thing that he could possibly say about God, the Virgin Mary, and the Bible. It disturbed me when I read it, but then I thought to myself, there are many members of the church that do not believe that hell is real either. They possibly would not say what this man has said, but they will laugh and joke about hell.

After I have left an individual who laughs and jokes about going to hell, suppose one of his friends were to come to him with the following message: "I have come to you, at the risk of my own life, so you listen carefully. I overheard a group of men plotting your death. Tonight that mob is coming to take your life. I heard them tell how they plan to kill you. They are going to burn your right hand from your arm, and then they are going to burn your left hand from that arm. After that they are going to burn your feet from your legs. Then they are going to hang you in a tree leaving you about five feet above the ground and build a fire under you. That is the way they are going to put you to death. That is the way you are going to die. And now, farewell, my friend."

Friends, if this were to happen, that same man who joked and laughed about going to a devil's hell, would leave his wife and children! He would swim rivers, cross deserts, and climb mountains to get away from that mob. Why? Because just the very thought of having the hand burned from his arm is more than he could stand. Yet he will laugh and joke about hell.

I am telling you, friends, you had better stop joking about hell, and ridiculing God! You say that you believe there is a hell and yet you reject the invitation. Are you really rational when you talk like that? Well, you had better think, my friend. That is the most terrible thing that could ever happen to an individual! Hell is not anything to joke about! When you say you are going to hell when you die it only means one thing, you do not believe there is such a place as hell. You cannot even strike a match and hold it to your finger, yet you laugh and joke about going to a place of outer darkness where the Bible says there is weeping and gnashing of teeth, where people will burn forever and forever. What is wrong with you? What has sin done to you? Sir, I can tell you of one person, tonight, who would tell you, "You had better believe that hell is real", because he is there this night and he said, "I am tormented in this flame." Listen to the following scriptures; do you believe them?

And these shall go away into everlasting punishment: but the righteous into life eternal (Matthew 25:46). Where the worm dieth not, and the fire is not quenched (Mark 9:44).

And the smoke of their torment ascendeth up forever and ever: and they have no rest day nor night, who worship the beast and his image, and whosoever receiveth the mark of his name (Revelation 14:11).

And the devil that deceived them was cast into the lake of fire and brimstone, where the beast and the false prophet are, and shall be tormented day and night forever and ever (Revelation 21:10).

But the fearful, and unbelieving, and the abominable, and murders, and whoremongers, and sorcerers, and idolaters, and all liars, shall have their part in the lake which burneth with fire and brimstone; which is the second death (Revelation 21:8).

He Learned It Was Too Late To Pray

You know, prayer is a wonderful thing in its place, but so many times an individual waits until it is too late to pray. I have heard a lot of sad prayers in my life. I have heard mothers pray over their wayward daughters, I have heard fathers pray over their prodigal sons. I have heard children pray at the open grave. I have heard them scream and ask why did God take their mother. Oh, I have heard prayers that would chill your blood.

I remember several years ago I was in a tent meeting in North Mobile. We baptized several people, among whom was a lady and her young son, about eleven years old. Somehow or other her husband could not see the need to render obedience unto the gospel. I remember going to his home and talking to him. But he did not see the importance of it. Within a few weeks he was stricken down. I went to the city hospital to see that man, and knew when I walked into the room that the light of life was just flickering in the socket. I remembered those gospel sermons that he heard. While I was talking to him his eleven-year-old boy came into the room. And when he did his father's eye caught him as he came in the door. He said, "Son, I want you to pray that your daddy may live." And that little boy went over and fell across the chest of his father, and prayed a prayer that would chill your blood. He prayed for God not to take his daddy away.

Oh, I have heard a lot of sad praying in my preaching life, prayers that would make you cry, but I have never heard anyone pray like the rich man prayed in hell. I want you to listen to his prayer. The Bible said he saw Abraham afar off and Lazarus in his bosom. He cried, "Father Abraham, have mercy upon me and send Lazarus," and now you listen to him, "that he may dip the tip of his finger in water, and cool my tongue; for I am tormented in this flame." Surely, surely, O God, you will not deny that. Surely, surely, this will be granted. I do not ask for a glass full. I am not asking for a spoonful of water. I am not even asking for a drop, so surely, surely, O God, he can come and take his damp finger and touch my tongue.

I never heard a prayer in my life that was sadder than that one. And the sad thing about it is that he is still praying, but without hope! Then you laugh and joke about hell, and say you know that you are going there. My friends, you had better come to your senses.

Abraham said to him, "Son do you not remember that back in the other world you had your good things?" And, my friends, that is what will haunt you in all eternity. One will hear those words, "Do you not remember, do you not remember, do you not remember those prophets, preachers, and teachers?" I say to you who have heard gospel sermons, if you die unprepared to meet God, you will recall every sermon you have heard preached. You do not need a book. No, no, my friends, you will not have to have a book to learn these sermons, because you will learn every one of them in hell and have an eternity to think about them.

The Bible says there is weeping and gnashing of teeth, and outer darkness. Just suppose in hell there is no more than a place of outer darkness. I read once about a boy who was lost in a cave for only 24 hours. When they found him they had to tie him, for he was raving mad. The darkness had driven him mad. You just think, if eternity were no more than some blasted continent of outer darkness where people would run and stumble and fall, and where a demon was sitting on every hill; where the wild animals were howling, and the serpents were hissing and the devils were groaning, that would be enough, seemingly more than a man could stand.

But hell is more than that. The Bible not only describes the place as outer darkness, but the Bible even pictures it as a bottomless pit. You have dreamed of falling, have you not? You fall, and fall, and fall, and then when you would awaken you would say, "Thank God, it was not real. It was only a dream." The Bible says that it is a bottomless pit. Five times in the book of Matthew hell is referred to as a place of weeping and gnashing of teeth. We have never suffered, nor has any man to the degree that one will suffer in hell.

History records that in 1777, when George Washington and his soldiers spent that bitter winter in Valley Forge, some of the soldiers had to have limbs amputated because of frost-bite. Relic hunters have recently found pieces of lead with impressions of teeth deeply imprinted therein. An old doctor's diary revealed how these impressions were made. When a soldier's arm or leg had to be amputated, the pain was so severe that they would tend to grind their teeth almost to powder during the ordeal. To prevent this, the lead was placed between their teeth.

The Bible pictures hell as a place of intense pain, a place of weeping and gnashing of teeth. You think about grinding and gnashing your teeth forever and ever. That is what hell is.

God does not want man to go there. He wants man to be saved. He does not want man to go to this place of outer darkness. I read once of a lady who had a parrot that she had taught to say a few words. Every night when she covered the cage she would say, "Good night" and turn the lights out. And over a period of weeks the parrot learned to say, "Good night" when the lights went out. In the morning when she would take the cover off the cage she would say, "Good morning." The parrot learned to say "Good morning" when the sun came up. One day the cat got hold of the parrot; though it was rescued before it was killed, its eyes were put out. That night when the lady put the cover over the cage she said, "Good night." The next morning when she took the cover off the cage she said, "Good morning," and the parrot said, "Good night." She said, "Good morning." The parrot said, "Good night." It never again said, "Good morning", because it was living in a world of darkness.

Hell is a place of outer darkness; of weeping and gnashing of teeth. It is a bottomless pit where all the bad, evil people of the world go. God does not want you to go there. He wants man to so live and conduct himself so that when he comes to the end of the way he can truthfully say, "I will not have to cross Jordan alone."

There are many who have spurned every invitation of Christ. We want you to confess your faith in Christ, and be baptized. So will you not come? We want you to do what others have already done—come to Jesus.

A SAD TIME WHEN GOD LAUGHS

This sermon preached at the Municipal Theatre in Anninston, Alabama 1968.

The subject that I have announced for this occasion is rather a shocking subject that sounds paradoxical in so many ways, "A Sad Time When God Laughs."

In Psalms 2:1-4, the writher says,

> Why do the heathen rage, and the people imagine a vain thing? The kings of the earth set themselves, and the rulers take counsel together, against the Lord, and against his anointed, saying, Let us break their bands asunder, and cast away their cords from us. He that sitteth in the heavens shall laugh: the Lord shall have them in derision.

In Psalms 37:13, "The Lord shall laugh at him, for he seeth that his day is coming." In Psalms 59:8, "But thou, O Lord, shalt laugh at them; thou shalt have all the heathen in derision." In Proverbs 1:22-31,

> How long, ye simple ones, will ye love simplicity? and the scorners delight in their scorning, and fools hate knowledge? Turn you at my reproof: behold, I will pour out my spirit unto you, I will make known my words unto you. Because I have called, and ye refused; I have stretched out my hand, and no man regarded: But ye have set at naught all my counsel, and would none of my reproof: I also will laugh at your calamity; I will mock when your fear cometh: When your fear cometh as desolation, and your destruction cometh as a whirlwind; when distress and anguish cometh upon you. Then shall they call upon me, but I will not answer; they shall seek me early, but they shall not find me. For that they hated knowledge, and did not choose the fear of the Lord. They would none of my counsel: They despised all my reproof. Therefore shall they eat of the fruit of their own way, and be filled with their own devices.

Four times God is pictured in the Bible as the laughing God. Ordinarily, we do not think of God laughing. We associate laughter with trivial, foolish, silly things. Since we cannot think of God as being frivolous, silly, or trivial we cannot associate laughter with God. But the Bible does picture God laughing. In every instance where God is pictured as the laughing God, the context of the verse shows that it was a sad time in the history of the world.

Man has always laughed at God. Yet man only laughs when he is on the pinnacle of victory. For instance, man does not laugh when his house is being burned to the ground. Man does not laugh when his plane is being hurled to the ground. Man does not laugh when his ship is going down at sea, thousands of miles from the closest island. Man does not laugh when his loved one is lying in a coma. Man does not laugh when his child is burning with fever and suffering with pain. Man does not laugh when he follows the casket of a loved one to the open grave. Man does not laugh when bombs are falling from the sky, killing and destroying people. Man does not laugh when cruel men are marching through the land murdering, burning, and destroying.

Man Laughs at God

Man only laughs when he is on the pinnacle of victory, when everything is going his way. Men have always laughed at God because they have made themselves believe that they can live without God. The philosophers laugh at God by putting themselves in the place of Jehovah. The state laughs at God by trying to stamp out religion. The atheist laughs at God by denying his very existence. The modernist laughs at God by denying the Virgin birth. The infidel laughs at God by trying to cut his word to threads. And the moralist laughs at God by teaching that man can be saved without rendering obedience unto the laws of God. And the mighty superman laughs at God by teaching that man can be saved by his own works, by his own morality, by his own goodness. Thus we see that from the early morning of time, man has laughed at Jehovah.

Now, I have mentioned these things because it is only natural to wonder why God would laugh. Let us get in mind first of all that man has always laughed at God. Every sinner living laughs at God. Every unfaithful church member laughs at God, otherwise, he would render obedience to Jehovah. Some of the things you hear me say may sound drastic, but I want you to keep in mind that man has always laughed at God.

God Laughs at Man

What is it that would motivate Jehovah to laugh at man? First, he does not laugh because he hates man. For in John 3:16 we are told that "God so loved the world that he gave his only begotten Son that whosoever believeth in him should not perish but have everlasting life." We cannot, with our finite minds, fully grasp this love. I am sure that I have never loved anyone like that. Notice that God "so" loved. No one knows the definition of the word "so" in this verse. Let us call upon the surveyors; let them survey the word. Let them tell us what it means. And they are not able to do it. Let those that make charts and maps draw a chart or map of the word "so", and tell us what it means. Man with his finite mind cannot do it. Let the astronomers who look out into space until the imagination of man staggers, tell us what the word "so" means. They are not able to do it.

The Bible says God "so" loved the world that he gave his only begotten Son. Just suppose that some dreaded disease should strike the world, a disease that kills man almost instantly. Newspaper headlines are dominated by reports of this tragedy. Suppose you read that every person in Japan had died, then every individual in China. You read of country after country where every living being has died. People are praying, scientists are searching, and the people of America fear the disease will strike this country. If it does, we know there is no hope, we will die. Then the tragic news comes that it has hit the West coast. Every individual in San Francisco died last week. The disease is coming this way. Have you ever thought how that would disturb you? Have you ever thought how often we would be going to the church building, praying to God? Why, we would hope and pray and pray that something might be done!

Finally researchers discover that if they can find one man who does not have the symptoms of this dreaded disease they can draw the blood from his body, make a serum, and save the rest of the people. But they have examined literally hundreds of millions of people and everybody has the symptoms. Then finally they come to my house. They say, "Mr. Black, you know why we are here. We are examining millions of people. We are trying to find one person who does not have the symptoms of this dreaded disease." They examine me and then they just frankly tell me that unless something is done in a few days I will die. They say that I have the symptoms. They examine my daughter, and say, "Within a few days she will die." Then they examine my son, and I observe that they go back and they examine him again and again. I see the doctor smile; I hear him talking to the nurse. Finally he says, "Mr. Black, we have found a boy who does not have the symptoms. He is your son. Now we cannot take him against your will. We can take your son and draw the blood from his body and we can save millions of people with his blood."

When I begin to think of that, I can, to some degree, appreciate the tremendous love that God had for me when the Bible says that God so loved the world that he gave his Son! The meaning of that verse is that God so loved you that he gave his Son that you might be saved. To every person in this beautiful municipal theater who has never rendered obedience unto the gospel, the meaning of that verse is this, that God so loved you that he gave his Son that you might have your sins forgiven. To every wayward church member it simply means that God so loved you that you might go to heaven when this life is over. Therefore I know that God does not laugh at man because he hates man; rather, he has a tremendous love for man, a love that we cannot grasp with our finite minds.

Secondly, I know that God does not laugh because he rejoices in man's impenitence, for in II Peter 3:9, the apostle Peter says, "The Lord is not slack concerning his promise, as some men count slackness; but is longsuffering to us-ward, not willing that any should perish, but that all should come to repentance." Our Lord wants every one to come to repentance. Actually, the Lord does not send anyone to the torments of hell. It is the Lord's will that all people be saved. And those who will not be saved are those who have trampled the law of God beneath their feet. When an individual tramples the law of God beneath his feet and dies in that condition, then this book pictures God as laughing at that individual.

God Laughs at the Futility of His Enemies

God laughs because he realizes that all his enemies are so weak and helpless. And if you are not a child of God, you are an enemy of God. Oh, no! You are not on neutral ground. You are either for Christ or against Christ. You will either accept Christ or you will reject Christ. You will not go away from this building the same individual you were when you came into the building. These words that we speak to you will either harden your heart or soften your heart, depending upon the attitude you have toward the word of God.

Have you ever thought just how futile man's efforts are? God made man with his own hands, stamped his own image upon him; yet puny man who is a worm of the dust then turns around and defies God, and tries to trample God beneath his feet. No wonder Job asked in Job 9:4, "He is wise in heart, and mighty in strength: who hath hardened himself against him, and hath prospered?" And I ask you, what man hath prospered who has hardened himself against God? Pharaoh tried that, but he did not prosper. Cain hardened himself against God, but he did not prosper. Those people in the cities of Sodom and Gomorrah hardened themselves against God, but they did not prosper. Hitler hardened himself against God, but he did not prosper. Mussolini hardened himself against God, but he did not prosper. And I am telling you, my friends, that when you harden yourself against God you are not going to prosper.

Now, every individual here has either been drawn closer to Christ or driven farther away. The Bible says that God hardened Pharaoh's heart. Pharaoh's heart was hardened because of the attitude that he had toward the word of God.

Can you conceive of an individual rejecting Christ in view of the invitation that Christ has extended? In Matthew 11:28-30, Jesus Christ said,

> Come unto me, all ye that labour and are heavy laden, and I will give you rest. Take my yoke upon you, and learn of me: for I am meek and lowly in heart; and ye shall find rest unto your souls. For my yoke is easy, and my burden is light.

Can you conceive of individual's rejecting Christ in view of his mission? In Luke 9:56 talking to James and John, Jesus said, "For the Son of man is not come to destroy men's lives, but to save them. And they went to another village." That was his very mission, his very purpose in coming to the earth, to save man from his sins.

Can you conceive of man's rejecting Christ in view of his authority? He said, "I have all power and all authority in heaven and on earth." Can you conceive of an individual rejecting Christ in view of his perfect life? There was never an individual who lived on this earth who could truthfully point a finger at the Son of God and say, "Thou art a sinner." He is the only person who has ever lived on this earth who was both God and man. He had concern for those who crucified him as he did those who followed him while here on earth. He was a perfect gentlemen from every standpoint. He was a perfect saint from every viewpoint. He never had an evil thought. He never spoke an ugly word. He never did an unkind deed. Now, can you conceive of man trying to trample him beneath his feet, yet wonder why the Bible says that God sits in the heavens and laughs at the people who are enemies of God?

I want to be perfectly frank with you, my friends, because we are all going to stand, before God on that day of judgment. I want to tell you the truth because I love you. You are not going to trample God beneath your feet and prosper. You are not going to harden yourself against God and be blessed. You are not going to boast yourselves against God and get by with it. This book teaches that God's enemies must be punished. Let me read it to you again in Psalms 37:13, "The Lord shall laugh at him: for he seeth that his day is coming." Just as surely as you are sinners this night, the Bible says the Lord is laughing at you for he knows your day is coming. Why, of course, you have laughed at God: every day of your life you laugh at God if you are not a Christian. But you must remember while you are laughing at God that the Bible says that God is laughing at you and is saying your day is coming. That simply means that there is going to be a pay-day some day. So God knows how futile his enemies are.

God Laughs Because He Can See the End of His Enemies

Then God laughed because he knows that all his enemies are going to be destroyed. If truth is going to win over error, righteousness over wickedness, God over Satan, then God's enemies must be destroyed. They cannot survive in God's world, so from the beginning of time God has always destroyed them. You remember that man had not lived upon the earth too long until he became wise in his own estimation and decided he would build a tower to heaven. I do not know how long they worked on this, maybe a week, maybe a month, maybe a year, but in my mind I can see God sitting on his throne up in heaven looking down upon these worms of the dust, and when he is fed up with it he laughs at them, confuses their languages so that when they ask for bricks they bring mortar, when they ask for mortar they bring water, when they ask for water they bring straw. What is God doing? He is laughing at these people. He is destroying them.

When man had lived upon the earth about 1600 years, we are told in Genesis 6:6-7,

> And it repented the Lord that he had made man on the earth, and it grieved him at his heart. And the Lord said, I will destroy man whom I have created from the face of the earth; both man, and beast, and the creeping thing, and the fowls of the air; for it repenteth me that I have made them.

And when God looked upon these people in that condition he sent the great baptismal flood and destroyed all his enemies. When the people in Sodom and Gomorrah became exceedingly wicked, what did God do? He sat in the heavens and laughed at them and destroyed them. When he sent Moses down into the land of Egypt to bring his people out of Egyptian bondage, and Pharaoh refused to let them go, what did God do? He destroyed Pharaoh and his army. God has always destroyed his enemies. When old Sennacherib sinned against God on one occasion, we are told that God slew 185,000 of his men. On another occasion when some people sinned against God he just opened up the earth and let them fall through and then covered the earth up over them. When old Nebuchadnezzar sinned against God, God laughed at him and made him become like a beast of the field, so that he ate grass like a wild animal. He has always destroyed his enemies, and I am telling you that if you are an enemy of God you are going to be destroyed just as sure as we are here.

It is said that Julian the Apostate tried to revive paganism in the Roman Empire after Constantine died, and he was wounded in battle. As he lay dying he caught some of his blood in his own hands and threw that blood toward heaven and said, "O Galilean, thou hast conquered." An truer words were never spoken. And I tell you that the man from Galilee is going to conquer again. And if you have set battle against God, you are going to be defeated. God is going to strike you down. He has always destroyed his enemies. He must destroy his enemies. He has no alternative. One of the saddest things in the world is for a man to make himself believe that he is in accord with God when in reality he is not.

In Proverbs 14:12, we read these words, "There is a way which seemeth right unto a man, but the end thereof are the ways of death." Every man's ways are right in his own eyes. Regardless of what a man may be religiously, he is right in his own eyes. But I am not asking, "Are you right in your own eyes?" I am asking you, "Are you right with the teachings of this book?"

Why it is said of Napoleon Bonaparte that he actually believed that he was protected by some supernatural power. Even though he shed rivers of blood, even though he made thousands of widows and orphans, he still believed that he was protected by some supernatural power. It is said that on the very night before the battle of Waterloo, he was riding through the dark as black as blackness itself, through a heavy thunderstorm. Beside him was one of his generals who happened to be looking in Napoleon's direction at the instance when lightning flashed. He later said, "Napoleon was looking toward the heavens and I heard him say, 'We are in accord'." But poor Napoleon! He read the elements wrong. And all that I ask you is, how many, how many, have read the elements wrong? How many have made themselves believe that they are in accord with God, when in reality they are not in accord with God?

You cannot be in accord with God, my friend, unless you have obeyed the teachings of this book. We have emphasized night after night during this campaign that in every example of conversion recorded in the book of Acts after the church of our Lord was set up, the sinner believed on Christ, repented of his sins, confessed his faith in

Christ and was baptized into Christ for the remission of his sins. The man who has not done this is not in accord with God. He cannot be in accord with God without doing this because it is God's law. Now he may be right in his own eyes. He may be like Napoleon; he may be reading the elements, but, brother, he may be reading the elements wrong. All of God's enemies are going to be destroyed. Your hope and my hope is to become a child of God so that we will not be destroyed.

God Laughs Because of the Security of His Cause

And then again God laughs because of the security of his cause. If you remember when the apostle Peter was speaking on the day of Pentecost, preaching the first gospel sermon ever to be preached under the world-wide commission, he spoke to those Jews about God's raising Christ from the dead. He told them that Jesus Christ was seated on David's throne by the right hand of God. Have you ever observed what else Peter told them? In Acts 2:23-24, you listen to it. He said,

Him, being delivered by the determinate counsel and foreknowledge of God, ye have taken, and by wicked hands have crucified and slain: Whom God hath raised up having loosed the pains of death: Because it was not possible that he should be holden of it.

There is no doubt that when the Jews crucified the son of God; when they took him down from that cross, a bloody corpse, and carried him away to the grave; no doubt they clapped their hands and said, "This is the last we will ever hear of this man. He is dead. If he had been the Son of God he would have come down from the cross." But Peter said that God raised him from the dead.

He said, "He was delivered to you by the determinate counsel and foreknowledge of God." You people did not upset the plans of God. That did not lessen their guilt, because if they had been reading what is known to us as the Old Testament—to them the scriptures—they would have known that in those scriptures the prophets talked about this Christ, told about his death and even about the very life he would live, and the very words he would utter while hanging on Calvary's cross. They told how he would be buried with the rich, raised on the third day. No wonder Peter said, "He was delivered to you by the determinate counsel and foreknowledge of God." That was Peter's way of saying to those people on the day of Pentecost that everything is going according to plan.

I can tell you something, my friends, if you could receive a communique from heaven, I can tell you just exactly what he would say. "Oh," but someone says, "Brother Black, this world is in a terrible condition, is it not?" Oh, yes, it is in a terrible condition. War clouds are hanging low; nation rising up against nation; men thirsting for power and authority. Oh, this world is in a terrible condition, but let me tell you something, my friend; this book teaches that all things are going according to plan. So if you could receive a communique from heaven tonight, I can tell you what it would say, "All things are going according to plan."

Regardless of the condition of the nuclear weapons that man may build, and regardless of the power that man may be able to generate; I know that God's eternal plan is that those who obey him are safe, regardless of what happens to the world, and those who disobey him will be lost regardless of what happens to this world. Man is not able to upset the plan of God. No, I do not know what the future may hold, but I know who holds the future. And I can simply say to you that all things are going according to plan.

God Laughs Because His Cause is Victorious

Then in the conclusion, God laughs because his cause is victorious. We often read of meetings of leaders of nations of the world and the message is about like this: "The meeting ended in a stalemate." That just means that they did not accomplish anything. But let me tell you something, my friend, your differences with your God are not going to end in a stalemate.

Jesus Christ did not come to the earth with the speculation of destroying the works of the devil. He came with the full assurance from God that he would do it. In I John 3:8, John said, "He that committeth sin is of the devil; for the devil sinneth form the beginning. For this purpose the Son of God was manifested, that he might destroy the works of the devil." In Philippians 2:8-11, the apostle Paul says,

> And being found in fashion as a man, he humbled himself, and became obedient unto death, even the death of the cross. Wherefore God also hath highly exalted him, and given him a name which is above every name: That at the name of Jesus every knee should bow, of things in heaven, and things in earth, and things under the earth; And that every tongue should confess that Jesus Christ is Lord, to the glory of God the Father.

Yes, my friends, God is going to be victorious in this thing. No wonder the Bible says then, "He that sitteth in the heavens shall laugh at them."

The question is, "At whom does God laugh?" First of all, at his avowed enemies. Listen to what he says, "The rulers of the earth have set themselves against the Lord." Can you conceive of that? Who has set themselves against the Lord? Well, let us see who they are that say, "Let us break the bands and cast the cord away from us." Well, what is wrong? The band is too tight and the writer here says, that the time would come that the people would take counsel against the anointed one and they would say, let us break the bands and cast the cord away from us. In other words these restrictions that God has bound upon us are too tight. Thus you hear people talk after this fashion today: "Do you mean to tell me that one has to do that? Do you mean to tell me that if a man does not do that he will lose his soul?" What is he doing? He has set himself against God. He is saying, "Let us break the band of God. The restrictions are too tight; we do not like that." And I say to you that we are living in an age when those very things are being fulfilled. Even religious people are trying to break the bands of God. How often have you discussed the Bible with an individual who would simply say, "I know the Bible says that, BUT . . " What does he mean by that? He simply means that even though God stated his will he is going to break the bands of God!

No man will tell you, for instance, that Jesus Christ did not command baptism. Every religious teacher in our town will tell us that Jesus Christ said do it. What is that man doing? He is attempting to break the band of God, the very thing that the writers said hundreds of years before Jesus Christ was born. And when a man is trying to break the band of God, He that sitteth in the heavens is laughing at him and saying, "Your day is coming."

The Lord laughs at those who laugh at his teaching. How many times have you tried to teach an individual the truth, maybe upon the subject of the church? One may turn to Matthew 16:18 and read what Jesus says, "And I say also unto thee, That thou art Peter, and upon this rock I will build my church: and the gates of hell shall not prevail against it." Also one may read Ephesians 4:1-6 where Paul says,

> I therefore, the prisoner of the Lord, beseech you that ye walk worthy of the vocation wherewith ye are called, with all lowliness and meekness, with longsuffering, forbearing one another in love;

Endeavouring to keep the unity of the Spirit in the bond of peace. There is one body, and one Spirit, even as ye are called in one hope of your calling; One Lord, one faith, one baptism, one God and Father of all, who is above all, and through all, and in you all.

By the time you read these verses the individual begins to chuckle. To him this is funny. He will ask, "Now do you mean by that that you believe there is just one church?" Why, that is his way of laughing at God! He is doing the very thing that David said he would do. He said the time will come when they will set themselves against God; then will try to break the band of God.

How many times have you tried to talk to an individual about baptism and you turn to the Bible and read where Jesus Christ said in Mark 16:15-16, "And he said unto them, Go ye into all the world, and preach the gospel to every creature. He that believeth and is baptized shall be saved, but he that believeth not shall be damned." Now you turn to Acts 2:38, "Then Peter said unto them, Repent, and be bapized every one of you in the name of Jesus Christ for the remission of sins, and ye shall receive the gift of the Holy Ghost." Now listen to Galatians 3:27: "For as many of you as have been baptised into Christ have put on Christ." In Acts 10:48 we also read, "And he commanded them to be baptized in the name of the Lord. Then prayed they him to tarry certain days." After reading these verses, what does some individual do? He laughs and ask, "Do you mean baptism is essential to salvation?"

Every Man Either Laughs At God Or Obeys God

Every man in this audience will either laugh at God or obey God while we sing the invitation. There are scores of people in this audience who have never accepted Christ. You may give a score of reasons for your hostility to Christ, such as the incredibility of miracles, the faults of Christians, but the final reason for your rejection is to be found in those laws of truth and love and purity which regulate His kingdom, and which are bright as gold and soft as silk to the righteous, but which are to the disobedient and lawless as hateful as the hangman's noose. Why reject Him? It is a vain, foolish act. To all His enemies we ask, what evil hath He done to you?

Statesmen are against Him, and yet they cannot shut their eyes to the fact that His religion makes grand nations. Philosophers are against Him, and yet they cannot deny that he has lighted up the intellectual sphere with a most precious and bright light. Moralists are against Him, and yet they confess His character to be unique and unapproachable in its sublimity and beauty and goodness. All sinners are against Him, and yet in their heart they know Him to be love, His law to be right, His kingdom to be the kingdom of heaven. To oppose Christ is madness, blind passion, suicidal folly, for He is the sinner's friend, the desire of the nations. It is not reasonable to reject Christ. All the raging of the unbelieving fails to destroy the truths of God. The ungodly storm and rage against the pious, excite all their counsel against them. But all this is as the stormy, swollen waves of the sea, which rush along as if they would break down the shore, but before they reach the shore they calm down again, vanish in themselves, or break up with a little foam upon the shore.

It is so hard to understand how people can reject this Christ. There are many in this audience who have rejected every invitation extended to you. Your rejection of Jesus Christ is after this order: First, you begin to think about submitting to Christ, then you postpone without any intention of submitting to Christ. The next step is for you to disregard, hear without heeding, then you begin to dislike what you hear and start turning away from the truth. Then you begin to actually hate the truth, cherishing a feeling of rebellious aversion; all this will end in mockery and scorn. When this happens in your life God will leave you alone. Hosea 4:17, "Ephraim is joined to idols; let him alone." Psalms 18:41, "They cried, but there was none to save them: even unto the Lord, but he answered them not." Romans 1:26, "For this cause God gave them up unto vile affections: for even their women did change the natural use into that which is against nature."

Will you come to Jesus? Someone has said, "Fools do at last what wise men do at first." I know that there is a battle going on within your own mind. I know that Satan is saying to you that you do not have courage enough to walk down the aisle before these people. On the other hand Jesus Christ is saying, "Come unto me all ye that labor and are heavy laden and I will give you rest." This is a decision you must make, no one else can make it for you. There are many who would do it for you if they could. I would do it for you if I could, but his is a decision you will have to make yourself. There are many on the first floor and many in the balcony who ought to accept Christ tonight. Will you not come while we sing this great invitation, "O Why Not Tonight"?

THE LAST DAY WHEN THE WONDERFUL BOOK WILL BE OPENED

This lecture delivered at Fort Worth Christian College, 1971,
Fort Worth, Texas.

But the day of the Lord will come as a thief in the night; in the which the heavens shall pass away with a great noise, and the elements shall melt with fervent heat, the earth also and the works that are therein shall be burned up. Seeing then that all things shall be dissolved, what manner of persons ought ye to be in all holy conversation and godliness, looking for and hastening unto the coming of the day of God, wherein the heavens being on fire shall be dissolved, and the elements shall melt with fervent heat? Nevertheless we, according to his promise, look for new heavens and a new earth, wherein dwelleth righteousness. Wherefore, beloved, seeing that ye look for such things, be diligent that ye may be found of him in peace, without spot, and blameless. (II Peter 3:10-14).

The judgment day is referred to in different ways.

But after thy hardness and impenitent heart treasurest up unto thyself wrath against the day of wrath and revelation of the righteous judgment of God (Rom. 2:15). For the great day of his wrath is come; and who shall be able to stand? (Rev. 6:17). Verily I say unto you, It shall be more tolerable for the land of Sodom and Gomorrah in the day of judgment, than for that city. (Matt. 10:15).

Many will say to me in that day, Lord, Lord, have we not prophesied in thy name? and in thy name have cast out devils? and in thy name done many wonderful works? (Matt. 7:22). And this is the Father's will which hath sent me, that of all which he hath given me I should lose nothing, but should raise it up again at the last day (John 6:39).

Every man's work should be made manifest: for the day shall declare it, because it shall be revealed by fire; and the fire shall try every man's work of what sort it is. (I Cor. 3:13).

Even though God has said much about this day, He has never made known to man when the day is coming. "But of that day and hour knoweth no man, no, not the angels of heaven, but my Father only" (Matt. 24:36).

The last day will be that great day when God will interpose directly into human history, and bring this old world to a final close. The Judge sitting on his throne will determine the eternal destiny of man. Every one will then go to that place adapted to his final condition.

THE LAST DAY WILL BE THE GREATEST
DAY KNOWN TO MAN

There have been many great days in our lives—the day we married—the day the first child was born—the day the first grandchild was born—that day we were reunited with our loved ones after many days of separation. I can remember when I was a little boy living on a farm during the depression in North Alabama. My grandfather, a doctor, lived in Ashville, N. C. In those days North Carolina was a long way from Alabama, so my grandfather would come to see us about every two years. We would get a letter from our grandfather telling us that he planned to visit in the Spring after the snow and ice in the mountains had melted and before it got too hot in Alabama. After this letter was read, every day we would ask Papa and Mama when is Grandpa coming? We knew he was coming because he said he was coming. I believe Jesus is coming because he said he is coming. Even though my grandfather did not give the exact date of his coming, we knew he was coming and would start preparing, the very day we got the letter, for his arrival. Who was excited about my grandfather's visit? Not the city, not even the community, but only his family.

The world is not excited about the coming of the Lord on the last day. The world as a whole is not thinking about the coming of Christ because they care nothing about Christ. Listen with what authority the Bible speaks along these lines.

> But the day of the Lord will come as a thief in the night; in the which the heavens shall pass away with a great noise, and the elements shall melt with fervent heat, the earth also and the works that are therein shall be burned up (II Pet. 3:10). Watch ye therefore: for ye know not when the master of the house cometh, at even, or at midnight, or at the cock crowing, or in the morning: Lest coming suddenly he find you sleeping. And what I say unto you I say unto all, watch (Mk. 13:37).

> But as the days of Noah were, so shall also the coming of the Son of man be. For as in the days that were before the flood they were eating and drinking, marrying, and giving in marriage, until the day that Noah entered into the ark, and knew not until the flood came, and took them all away; so shall also the coming of the Son of man be (Matt. 24:37-39).

On that dreadful night of August 17, 1969 when the Gulf Coast of Mississippi was destroyed by the hurricane Camille, hundreds of people died, even though they had plenty of time to escape. They simply did not believe that they would be destroyed because they refused to heed the warning. In one large house twenty-two young people were having a party and the policemen went there three times warning them; they simply laughed because they were having a good time, and did not believe the warning. They suddenly realized death was closing in on them but it was too late.

This day of which our text speaks is called "the day of the Lord" because for it all other days have been made, from it all other days borrow their value, and into it the interest of all other days will be crowded, from the first day that dawned and flashed its splendors upon man's Eden home till the last day shall fade. It will be emphatically, "The day of the Lord," because then Christ will so publicly demonstrate His justice and integrity in saving the righteous and destroying the wicked, as to call forth the voluntary and spontaneous sanction of the universe.

THE DAY THE DEAD WILL BE RAISED

All of us are concerned about death. For out there in that lonesome valley or by a mountain side or on some far away battle-field lies the bodies of those who are dear to us.

> And not only they, but ourselves also, which have the first fruits of Spirit, even we ourselves groan within ourselves, waiting for the adoption, to wit, the redemption of our body. (Rom. 8:23). Being grieved that they taught the people, and preached through Jesus the resurrection from the dead. (Acts 4:2).

Christ also taught by words and actions that the resurrection of the body was included in the great work of which he was the subject. There was a pleasant little family in the town of Bethany, nearly two miles from Jerusalem, that Jesus loved. This family was composed of two sisters and one brother. In the absence of Jesus, Lazarus died and was buried in a cave and covered with a stone. Jesus heard of it, and he and his disciples started for the scene of mourning, and arrived at Bethany four days after the funeral service and burial. Before he entered the town, Martha heard of his coming and went to meet him. When Martha met him she said, "Lord, if thou hadst been here, my brother had not died." Jesus said, "Thy brother shall rise again."

Martha said, "I know he shall rise again in the resurrection at the last day." Jesus said, "I am the resurrection and the life."

Mary also ran to meet Jesus and fell down at his feet and said, "Lord if thou hadst been here my brother had not died." Mary wept, the Jews who had followed her wept, and "Jesus wept." Jesus asked, "Where have ye laid him?" They go to the grave and it was here that Jesus cried with a loud voice, which one day will pour its trumpet thunders throughout the vast charnel house of the dead and bid us all live, "Lazarus, come forth." When those words were spoken the pulse of immortality began its vibration in the grave, and the sheeted dead came forth alive.

That one dead man made alive again argues that all dead men shall be raised; that Jesus raised him from the dead during his redemptive mission on earth is conclusive that the resurrection is embraced in the work of redemption. That the death heard and obeyed him once, aruges that death will hear and obey him again. This conclusion is clear from the fact that when Jesus was completing redemption's plan the graves were opened, and "many bodies of the saints which slept arose and came out of the graves." It is true that one day our bodies will be placed between the silent halls of death. Paul said, "This corruptible must put on incorruption and this mortal must put on immortality." The Lord shall change our vile body. His body shall be our model.

The righteous will then realize that this is the day of all days and that it is the most wonderful, glorious and happiest day that they have ever known and this will be the day that they will join hands with all of the redeemed of all ages and gather around that great white throne and sing that great song that John heard on Patmos, "Thou wast slain and hath redeemed unto God by the blood from every tongue, kindred and nation." (Rev. 5:9).

THE LAST DAY GOD'S WRATH WILL BE
MANIFESTED TOWARD THE WICKED

God is angry with the sinner every day. The writer of Psalms tells us that the sinner walks in slippery places and always exposed to fall. (Ps. 73:18). He does not know but what he may fall the next minute. When the sinner does fall in death, he will be cast into hell. The hand of man cannot be strong when God rises up. The strongest have no power to resist him. There is no fortress that is any defense from the power of God. Though hand in hand the vast multitudes of God's enemies may unite their forces, they will be broken in pieces easily. The enemies of

God are as light chaff before the whirlwind of large quantites of dry stubble before devouring flames. It is easy for a man to crush a worm or cut a slender thread, thus it is easy for God, when he pleases to cast the sinner into hell.

How does the sinner think he can stand before the one who has power to pick the earth up and shake it like a blanket or can roll the heaven back like a scroll? The one who has the power to overturn mountains, upheave valleys and rupture strata? This is the one who will damn sinners to an eternal hell. The sinner deserves to be cast into hell. The devil is watching every sinner, he stands like a greedy hungry lion watching for his prey. The old serpent is gaping for them, hell opens its mouth wide to receive them, and if they don't repent they will be hastily swallowed up and lost. The souls of the wicked are compared to the troubled sea. "But the wicked are like the troubled sea, when it cannot rest, whose waters cast up mire and dirt." (Is. 57:20).

"For, behold, the Lord will come with fire, and with his chariots like a whirlwind, to render his anger with fire, and his rebuke with flames of fire." (Isa. 66:15). The wrath of God, how dreadful! But it is more, the fury of God! The fierceness of Jehovah! Oh, how dreadful must this be! Who can utter or conceive what expressions are carried in them! But it is also "the fierceness and wrath of Almighty God." To what a dreadful, inexpressible, inconceivable depth of misery must the poor creature be sunk who shall be the subject of God's wrath. Every person who has never obeyed the gospel is hanging over the pit of hell by a thin string that is almost ready to snap.

THE DAY THE BOOKS WILL BE OPENED

It is interesting to observe how often books are connected with the judgment.

> Yet now, if thou wilt forgive their sin—; and if not, blot me, I pray thee, out of thy book which thou hast written. (Ex. 32:32). A fiery stream issued and came forth from before him: thousand thousands ministered unto him, and ten thousand times ten thousand stood before him: the judgment was set, and the books were opened. (Dan. 7:10). Notwithstanding in this rejoice not, that the spirits are subject unto you, but rather rejoice, because your names are written in heaven. (Luke 10:20).

> And I saw the dead, small and great, stand before God; and the books were opened: and another book was opened, which is the book

of life: and the dead were judged out of those things which were written in the books, according to their works. And the sea gave up the dead which were in it; and death and hell delivered the dead which were in them: and they were judged every man according to their works. And death and hell were cast into the lake of fire. This is the second death. And whosoever was not found written in the book of life was cast into the lake of fire. (Rev. 20:12-15). And there shall in no wise enter into it anything that defileth, neither whatsoever worketh abomination or maketh a lie: but they which are written in the Lamb's book of life. (Rev. 21:27).

When the books are opened, all will be present to be judged by the law under which they lived. The persecutors of the righteous, the crucifiers of the Lord and the enemies to all that is good will stand as trembling culprits at his judicial bar. All the ungodly will stand quaking beneath the majesty of His glory. The wicked will realize that the administration of grace has come to an end. All the angels will be there. Those in places of torment will be there. Those in places of rest and contentment will be there. Every son and daughter of our apostate race will be there. All who lived before us since Adam will be there. All those who live after us until that trumpet of God shall sound will be there. What an intergrated audience!

The judge will then be seated on His great white throne and will open at last the books. He takes the books, my book, that records my life; your book, that records your life, and the Lamb's book of life and that wonderful book the Bible, and we will be judged. Christ, now, will have on his judicial robe, for the redemptive robe has been laid aside and never to be worn again. Sinners will fall upon their knees and with streaming eyes lift their heads to heaven, and plead for pardon and salvation, but the mediatorial work of Christ will have come to an end, the dispensation of grace will be finished, and mercy to the disobedient will be gone forever.

On the left hand we see unbelievers, idolatores, murderers, drunkards, robbers, adulterers, blasphemers, liars, slanderers, misers, worldly minded hypocrites, lukewarm professors, apostates, ministers who worked too little, ministers who neglected to feed the sheep, ministers who preached themselves instead of preaching Christ. These on the left hand will hear these awful words, "Depart ye cursed into the hell prepared for the devil and his angels."

On the right hand we see those who were once orphans and widows; those who were once persecuted for righteousness sake;

ministers with stars in their crowns, and the redeemed of all ages will live with Jesus forever. These will hear those wonderful words, "Come ye Blessed."

THE DAY ETERNITY SETS IN

This awful word, "eternity" is found only one time in the Bible.

> For thus saith the high and lofty One that inhabiteth eternity, whose name is Holy; I dwell in the high and holy place, with him also that is of a contrite and humble spirit, to revive the spirit of the humble, and to revive the heart of the contrite ones. (Isa. 57:15).

To the faithful child of God the word eternity is a beautiful word but for the wicked it is a dreadful word. Man with his finite mind cannot fully comprehend it. Eternity is as high and wide and deep as God.

I can tell you what time is, but eternity cannot be defined. Time can be measured, because it is first measured by the revolutions of the planets and the aspect of the stars; because having a beginning and an end its past can be increased, and its future diminished. It can be defined because it has parts, these parts sustain relationships to each other and the whole. But eternity cannot be defined. Beginningless and endless it cannot be measured, its past increased, its future diminished. It has no past, it has no future, it has no end, it has no middle, it has no parts.

Eternity is an infinite line. If the strongest winged angel of heaven could fly in one direction for a billion years, that angel could no more find the end of eternity than he could find the cradle or tomb of the Almighty God. It is a day without a morning, a day without an evening. It was high noon when the world was made, it will be noon when the world is destroyed—it will be high noon forever. O eternity! The idea deepens, widens and towers, till the human mind, confounded and crushed, cries, "O eternity, tell us thy name." All languages beg at thy footstool, tell us thy name. O eternity, how dreadful when joined to the penalty of sin.

WHAT MANNER OF PERSON OUGHT YE TO BE

"Seeing then that all these things shall be dissolved, what manner of persons ought ye to be in all holy conversation and godliness." (2 Pet. 3:11). We should ask ourselves this question often in view of the judgment.

We should be a people unspotted from the world. Keeping ourselves unspotted from the world consists of more than simply meeting together for prayer, singing hymns and hearing sermons. These are wonderful but many other things are important. It is by only maintaining a vigorous spiritual life that we can hope to keep ourselves "unspotted from the world." We are living in an age when people seem to find sin hilariously funny. I ask you, what is funny about open immorality, broken homes, orphan children, crowded hospitals, murderous highways or the world's juvenile delinquency?

If a man is to keep himself unspotted from the world, he must realize that sin is the worst thing in God's universe. Sin brings fear, and sin destroys. (Gen. 3:9-11; Ps. 73:19).

In First John we are told not to love the world.

> Love not the world, neither the things that are in the world. If any man love the world, the love of the Father is not in him. For all that is in the world, the lust of the flesh, and the lust of the eyes, and the pride of life, is not of the Father, but is of the world. And the world passeth away, and the lust thereof: but he that doeth the will of God abideth forever. (1 Jn. 2:15-17).

The love of God and the love of the world are diametrically opposed to each other; and no one is acceptable to God who allows the world to have first place in his heart. I am aware of the fact that it is not always easy to define the boundaries of worldliness. Ignorance and bigotry pronounce many things wrong which are harmless; on the other hand carelessness and laxity permit many things which are by no means innocent. The only way to be certain in this matter is to determine the principles which govern such issues, and always act on that basis. Worldliness does not consist only in doing certain things or being in certain places. It can be a state of mind. It is possible for one to be in a church building where people are singing, praying and engaging in other acts of worship, yet his mind may be a thousand miles away; this is worldliness. Yes, worldliness can be a state of mind. And in view of the judgment day we must keep ourselves unspotted from the world.

In view of the judgment we should be zealous people. It is possible even for a church to drift into a lukewarm position. The church in Laodicea was not disturbed by hereasies or broken up by persecution; there was no one of a contentious disposition; they had drifted into an easy going way of living. No one in the church, as far as I know, brought any disgrace upon the Christian name. They were neither earnest for God, nor utterly indifferent to religion. They worshipped their idol of good taste, or good form, and looked upon enthusiasm, no doubt, as ill-bread and disturbing. They never put themselves to any inconvenience, braved any reproach, or abondoned any comfort for Christ's sake. They kept pace with the world and flattered themselves that they stood well with God. Carlyle called this the hypocrisy which does not know itself to be hypocritical.

The brethren were not cold, but they were not hot; they were not infidels, yet they were not earnest believers; they did not oppose the gospel neither did they defend it. They were not working mischief neither were they doing any great good; they were not disreputable in moral character, but they were not distinguished for holiness; they were not irreligious, but they were not enthusiastic in piety.

This church, no doubt, had elders and deacons who were excellent pillars of the church, if the chief function of a pillar is to stand still and exhibit no motion or emotion. They, no doubt, had ministers, but their wings had been clipped for they did not fly very far in preaching the gospel.

Men are less apt to repent in the "middle of the road" position, between hot and cold, than if they were in the worst extremes of sin. If they had been like Saul of Tarsus, an enemy of Christ, they might be converted, but they were the Gamaliel, neither opposing nor favoring. In view of the fact that we will stand on the last day and see that wonderful book opened, we ought to be a zealous, dedicated people, promoting goodness and righteousness in this sin cursed world.

At the last day the Lord will come to receive his saints. Even though our Christian friends must die, we should not engage in great sorrow. We are the offspring of God, and God is the Father of our spirits. Our spirits are immortal. When death enters the family circle, and with its cold breath kisses to sleep some of our loved ones and bears them from us, we are prone to bow our heads like the ripened grain, and array ourselves in mourning; the heart is sore, and the voice is broken; smiles are banished from our faces, and joy from our hearts. But we must remember that which we commit to the tomb is not the loved one, it is only the house in which our loved one lived. To a Christian death is not a calamity, it is but the gateway, the vestibule to the eternal home, where pain and sorrow are unknown. Death breaks that dark prison in which the man dwells and allows the spirit to unfold its wings and fly away to those celestial mansions that await those who love the Lord.

THE WAY — THE CHURCH

This Lecture delivered at Harding College, Searcy, Arkansas.

Among the many laudable, commendable and philanthropic institutions organized for the elevation of man, none can claim equality with or superiority over the divine institution—the church of the Lord Jesus Christ. What the sun is to the planetary system—the church is to the world.

The church of Christ challenges all human institutions. It makes rich and does not bankrupt. The church proposes to do peaceably by love, unaided by force, more than huge armies can do by power of the sword. All human institutions for good, regardless of name, must stand back aghast in the hour of death unable to bridge the chasm over the dark valley. Here the church comes to the rescue and erects her banner on the other side of the grave. And on this banner are written in letters of gold, "I am the resurrection and the life: he that believeth on me, though he were dead, yet shall he live."

Jesus Christ steps into the grave, supplies the "wanting link," connects the visible with the invisible, bridges the chasm of death, and says to every believer, "Cross over on me." Nothing that men can possibly discover or invent can produce in the human heart an expectation, much less a hope, that he will live again. Here the world fails, and the way—the church, comes in triumphant over all.

We need to impress upon the minds of the people the urgent need of learning of the way—the church. While conditions may have changed materially for the better, other conditions have arisen which produce a more urgent need for the truth concerning the church. Once men were in a fog of confusion due to sectarian division and bitterness; they are in a denser fog today produced by philosophies and theories and confusion confounded. Hundreds of cults, social uplift schemes, materialistic programs of rabid atheistic propaganda thrust themselves upon the scene until men despair of knowing the truth. They turn to cynic indifference and fill their lives with worldly pleasures.

People generally are unaware that there is a simple, beautiful, understandable and God given way of life that leads to absolute assurance and guidance. If ever the plain preaching of the New Testament was needed concerning the way—the church, it is now. Men are weary with confusion and darkness, but endure it because they have never seen the light. There are millions of people who are now indifferent to and ignorant of this God given way, the church, who would gladly turn to it if they would but come to know the simple terms of pardon so clearly given in the New Testament. In every community, however intelligent the people may be, there are great numbers who know nothing of the plain New Testament way.

That the church was commonly referred to as "the way" is clearly shown by the following verses:

> Acts 9:2, And he desired of him letters to Damascus to the synagogues, that if he found any of this way, whether they were men or women, he might bring them bound unto Jerusalem, Acts 22:4, And I persecuted this way unto the death, binding and delivering into prison both men and women. Acts 24:14, But this I confess unto thee, that after the way which they call heresy, so worship I the God of my fathers, believing all things which are written in the law and in the prophets.

> Acts 24:22, And when Felix heard these things, having more perfect knowledge of that way, he deferred them, and said, when Lysias the chief captain shall come down, I will know the uttermost of your matter.

These verses teach us that in the early days of New Testament Christianity the church was commonly referred to as "the way." It was called the way because it originated with Him who called Himself the way. The church was called the way because it was composed of those who had obeyed the truth, and who were performing their duties as Christians and those who had obeyed and obtained the salvation which was in Christ. John 14:6 is the fundamental, central and crowning truth of the Bible. It is the master key which unlocks Revelation's riddle; it is the master hand which unravels its mysteries and weaves the disentangled threads into a beautiful web of consistent and comprehensible truth. It is the keystone hewn by our Immanuel out of the diamond rocks of heaven, and chiselled and polished by His artistic hand, while Calvary trembled beneath the blows of His weighty hammer which awakened the dead and frightened; created light back into the womb of uncreated night, and now finished and duplicated, glitters in the symmetric arches of the beautiful bridge of salvation stretching from the regions of death to the regions of life, spanning hell and Hades, its every stone cemented by the blood of its architect and builder.

There were many reasons why people spoke of the church during the lifetime of Paul as being the way.

This seems to have been the earliest name by which the disciples were called. That it was used as a distinctive appellation of the Christian religion is seen by the following verses:

> Acts 19:9, But when divers were hardened, and believed not, but spake evil of that way before the multitude, he departed from them, and separated the disciples, disputing daily in the school of one Tyrannus. Acts 19:23, And the same time there arose no small stir about that way. Acts 24:14, But this I confess unto thee, that after the way which they call heresy, so worship I the God of my fathers, believing all things which are written in the law and in the prophets. 2 Pet. 2:2, And many shall follow their pernicious ways; by reason of whom the way of truth shall be evil spoken of. Isa. 35:8, And an highway shall be there, and a way, and it shall be called the way of holiness; the unclean shall not pass over it; but it shall be for those: the wayfaring men, though fools, shall not err therein.

IT WAS A WAY OF ZEAL

The early church was not activated by traditional zeal, angry zeal, boastful zeal, misguided zeal, impure or superstitious zeal, but it was filled with Christian zeal. The early Christians did not satisfy themselves with just keeping up to a fair average level.

The early church realized that if God was worth serving at all, He was worth serving with zeal. They had a pure and fervent zeal that motivated them to take their stand with the few or even alone, if necessary, to cry out against all sorts of worldly principles and practices. Rom. 9:1-3. "I say the truth in Christ, I lie not, my conscience also bearing me witness in the Holy Ghost. That I have great heaviness and continual sorrow in heart. For I could wish that myself were accused from Christ for my brethren, my kinsmen according to the flesh." Such was an apostle's love. Great must have been his zeal for souls that God put into his heart such a thought as this, that he could bear even to be separated from him whom his soul loved so dearly, if greater glory could be gained. These early Christians realized that there was nothing in the world as precious as the soul of man redeemed by the blood of Christ. Because of this zeal for Christ they could not look upon the Lord's work with indifference. The zeal for Christ's work made them active and aggressive. Righteous zeal can no more remain long in the presence of evil without attacking it than a hungry lion in the presence of his prey, or a powerful army in the presence of the foe. Zeal will attack the walls of Jericho with ram's horns, go forth against a giant with a shepherd's sling, and cleanse the temple with a scourge of cords. Zeal has the voice of thunder, its deeds are like lightning, its words are like a two edged sword, and its chariots and horses are fire.

We must pattern our preaching after our Master and the apostles. If we in the last century had displayed the same zeal for Christ and His church that the apostle Paul and his contemporaries displayed, the church would have been saved much of its sad history, and so large portions of the world would not remain heathen. It is the duty of every Christian to rightly divide the truth, to learn the essentials of Christianity, and to do all within his power to make the truth known to the whole world. This Christian zeal that was characteristic of Paul and his co-workers was a steady, permanent force, not transient, not occasional, not flickering up into a vehement flame and then dying away again, but like the sun, moon, and stars, ever circling their central God, measuring everything not by itself but by the majesty of Him for whom it is done. No great worthy cause was ever brought to success and victory without zealous labors. A zealous spirit is essential to the success in anything.

The Lord despises indifference. In Rev. 3:14-19,

> And unto the angel of the church of the Laodiceans write; These things saith the Amen, the faithful and true witness, the beginning of the creation of God, I know thy works, that thou art neither cold nor hot; I would thou wert cold or hot. So then because thou art lukewarm, and neither cold nor hot, I will spew thee out of my mouth. Because thou sayest, I am rich, and increased with goods, and have need of nothing; and knowest not that thou are wretched, and miserable, and poor, and blind, and naked: I counsel thee to buy of me gold tried in the fire, that thou mayest be rich; and white raiment, that thou mayest be clothed, and that the shame of thy nakedness do not appear; and anoint thine eye with eyesalve, that thou mayest see. As many as I love, I rebuke and chasen: be zealous therefore, and repent.

This is a classic example of a church lacking in zeal. It was dying as churches can die, of moderation and respectability. It might, in its apparently sound and safe prosperity, be the envy of other churches. Its very evenness, its persistently keeping at a dead level, was supreme offence to Christ. Nobody in the church brought any disgrace upon the Christian name. The church did not make the holy and inspiring witness of consistency in keeping at a high level of Christian attainment and service. It was simply easeful, indifferent, content to go on, aiming and doing nothing. The lukewarm are neither earnest for God, nor utterly indifferent to religion. They are perhaps best described as those who take an interest in religion, but whose worship of their idol of good taste, or good form, leads them to regard enthusiasm as ill-bred and disturbing; and who never put themselves to any inconvenience, braved any reproach, or abondoned any comfort for Christ's sake, but hoped to keep well with the world, while they flattered themselves that they stood well with God. Carlyle calls it, "The hypocrisy which does not know itself to be hypocritical."

The people of Laodicea were not cold, but they were not hot; they were not infidels, yet they were not earnest believers; they did not oppose the gospel neither did they defend it. They were not working mischief, neither were they earnest believers; they did not oppose the gospel, neither did they defend it. They were not working mischief, neither were they doing any great good; they were not disreputable in moral character, but they were not distinguished for holiness; they were not irreligious, but they were not enthusiastic in piety nor motivated by zeal. They were what the world calls "moderates;" they were of the broad church school; they were prudent and avoided fanaticism, respectable and averse to excitement. Good things were maintained among them, but they did not make much of them; they had prayer meetings, but there were few present, for they liked quiet evenings at home. When more attended the meetings they were still very dull, for they did their praying very deliberately and they were afraid of being too excited. They were content to have all things done decently and in order, but vigor and zeal they considered to be vulgar. God has given us this information concerning the church at Laodicea to let us know how he feels toward the church that is not active in promoting His cause.

THE CHURCH WAS CALLED THE WAY
BECAUSE OF ITS MISSION WORK

The early church must have been impressed by Paul's statement in Romans 10:13-15,

> For whosoever shall call upon the name of the Lord shall be saved. How then shall they call on him in whom they have not believed? And how shall they believe in him of whom they have not heard? And how shall they hear without a preacher? And how shall they preach, except they be sent? As it is written, how beautiful are the feet of them that preach the gospel of peace, and bring glad tidings of good things !

When Paul wrote this epistle, the ancient Roman virtue, the admirable simplicity, and unconquerable courage had died away. The decay and corruption of it were accelerated by the engrafting of new and dark superstitions. Vice was deified. The pagan world knew not God. But when the gospel had reached them, it had a tremendous influence upon their lives. It purified their heart and made their conscience sensitive. Those who became Christians no longer practiced self-torment, devil worship, human sacrifice and slaughter of wives.

The early church felt keenly the responsibility of reporting the gospel to the whole world. They believed the report of the gospel to be divine in origin, unique in its character, authentic in its facts, authoritative in its statements and marvelous in its declarations.

Those who composed the way did not rely upon the wisdom of the philosophical teaching of the great. They put their faith in Christ and resolved to give the report of the gospel to the whole world.

This gospel gave a report on the life of Christ. The life of Christ which the gospel makes known has no parallel in the history of races. Christ's mysterious conception was grandly confirmed by his mysterious career, his unique birth; He was unique in everything he did. If just one link in his life could be found faulty, then all is faulty. But every link has been found a perfect link; the whole life wondrously consistent, complete and unrivalled. For more than nineteen hundred years this life has been stirring humanity to its very core and center.

The early church would not forget the command of Mark 16:15, "And he said unto them, Go ye into all the world, and preach the gospel to every creature." The apostles and their co-workers, those great giants of the cross, embarked on their sublime but hazardous enterprise; beginning at Jerusalem, they sailed forth to the regions beyond and preached Jesus and the resurrection. In less than one hundred years after they started the gospel had sounded its report all over the Roman empire, even in the ranks of Caesar's household. Yes, it is easy to see why the church was referred to as "the way."

The only organization for the evangelization of the world is the church. The task assigned being no light one, it follows that the church must be prepared to meet its obligation. One church, however well trained, cannot reach the whole world; but it can plant other churches, and they in turn plant other churches; by this method the whole world could be preached to in comparatively short time.

World evangelization began with a company of only twelve men which grew into a church of three thousand the first day. In a generation churches were planted all over the Roman empire, and the gospel became known to the whole world. The mission of the church is to turn the world from darkness to light, to convert a sin-lost and sin-ruined world from error, to lead them by the truth, the gospel, into the kingdom, the church of the Lord and Master. This the church must do, if it is to carry out the purpose of God and our Saviour. We must give out or give up. We must send or end. We must use or lose. The last words the apostles heard Jesus say while he was on earth were, "Unto the uttermost part of the earth."

Christianity is essentially a missionary system. There are altogether too many congregations that are not attempting to do anything in the way of preaching the gospel away from home.

THE CHURCH WAS CALLED THE WAY
BECAUSE OF ITS LOVE

If we were to describe Christianity to one who had never known anything about it, we probably could not find a better way than to use the words of Jesus in this statement, "I am the way, the truth, and the life." The expression "the way" emphasizes the fact that Christianity is a way of conduct. It is a religion of doing, of being, of going, not merely of accepting a certain set of ideas; it is a religion of action and experience. Christianity is the way, the highway of God, the way of righteousness, the way of salvation, the way to heaven. Too many people have confused church-anity with real Christianity. Too many people have thought that becoming a Christian consists of joining some religious party or denomination and depending upon certain prescribed services and paying of prescribed dues. They have looked on the matter of being a Christian in the very same light as they would look upon the matter of joining a civic club or P.T.A.

The Bible teaches that love is the way of Christ, that it is the way of the cross, that it is the way of the church that cost the life-blood of the Son of God. This is another reason that the early Christians were simply referred to as "the way." It was the way that was different, the way that completely transformed the lives of men and women.

How do people of the world identify us today? Is it because of the great love that we have for one another? I rather think the world identifies us by the fact we baptize by immersion and take the Lord's Supper every first day of the week. These things are well and good and ought to be practiced, but the world should be able to identify us by the great love we have one for each other. Love ought to be one of the outstanding marks of identification of the Lord's people. It is a common thing to detect, in most of the congregations, a lack of love on the part of many. This brother shuns that brother, and this sister has nothing to do with some other sister. All of these people meet to worship God and sing, "Oh, How I Love Jesus." There is not a word of truth in it, for how can we love Jesus and hate our brethren? How is the church where you worship identified?

Of all the identifying marks of the apostolic church, that of love was, no doubt, the one which attracted the most attention. Jesus pointed out that one distinct characteristic of His church would be that of love.

Jn. 13:35, By this shall all men know that ye are my disciples, if ye have love one to another. 1 Jn. 3:14-16, We know that we have passed from death to life, because we love the brethren. He that loveth not his brother abideth in death. Whosoever hateth his brother is a murderer: and ye know that no murderer hath eternal life abiding in him. Hereby perceive we the love of God, because he laid down his life for us: and we ought to lay down our lives for our brethren.

In 1 Corinthians thirteen Paul makes void every pretense of Christianity which is not motivated by love.

Historians tell us that even the heathen of the first century, upon observing the newly found church, would exclaim, "Behold! How they love one another." The Jew was known by his circumcision, the Pharisee by his dress, and even today, there are those religionists whose identity depend almost entirely upon their manner of dress or by some other physical peculiarity; however, every true Christian possesses the one trait for which the world sighs, love. Since the early years of the restoration movement our pleas have neglected, for the most part, the one distinguishing mark about which our Lord and the apostles had more to say than about any other thing . . .our plea, "speaking where the Bible speaks." Too long we have been contented with a movement distinguished by its "doctrinal" marks while barren in the works of love.

One of the reasons the church has been plagued and disturbed by hobbyists and false teachers in the last few years is because these hobbyists are lacking in love for God, the church and the brethren. A man barren in love gets a joy out of sowing discord.

John 13:34-35, A new commandment I give unto you, that ye love one another; as I have loved you, that ye also love one another. By this shall all men know that ye are my disciple, if ye have love one to another.

Christ said this was a new commandment.

1. It was new because of the extent of the love. We are to love our neighbor as ourselves, but we are to love our fellow Christian as Christ loved us, and that is far more than we love ourselves. Christ loved us more than he loved himself, for he gave himself for us. Now Christ says, "You love one another as I have loved you." A love like this was never enjoined by the Law of Moses.

2. It was a new commandment because it was backed by a new reason. The old commandment was backed by this declaration, "I am the Lord thy God, which brought thee out of the land of Egypt, out of the house of bondage." The Israelite was to obey the law because of the redemption which God had wrought for His nation in Egypt, but we are commanded to love one another because Christ has redeemed us from a far worse bondage than that of Egypt. They were redeemed with the blood of Christ.

3. It was a new commandment because it is a new love, springing from a new nature and embracing a new nature. I am bound as man to love my fellow man as a man, I am bound as a Christian to love my fellow Christian as a Christian because he is a Christian. The ties of grace are far stronger than the ties of blood. If we are sons of God, we are brothers by a brotherhood that is stronger than the natural brotherhood which enables us to lie in the same cradle and to have nursed at the same breast, for brothers according to the flesh may be separated forever, but our Christian brotherhood will last forever.

4. This was a new commandment because it was enforced by new necessities. We are a band of brothers in the midst of a vast multitude of enemies. We are like a company of soldiers in the enemy's country. We must be banded together by brotherly love. God grant that the very fact we are faced with so many enemies, we may all endeavor to keep the "unity of the spirit in the bond of peace."

When the church comes to exemplify love—love one toward another, and love toward our enemies, then and only then will the man on the street really be impressed with New Testament Christianity. This is the greatest way known to man, because:

1. It is a way of thinking. It is characteristic of Christianity that it has its own peculiar way of thinking about God, man, sin and redemption. Its way of thinking is placed under the guidance of special divine revelation and the starting point of its thinking is that God has, "in these last days spoken unto us by His son."

2. It is a way of feeling. Every true disciple is distinguished by his admiration for, his trust in, and his love for the Lord Jesus Christ. In the early church the loyalty and love were so strong that the disciples could endure shame and death for His sake. Our way of thinking about Christ should mark us off from all the world; men should "take knowledge of us that we have been with Jesus," that he has won our very hearts, and for us to live is Christ.

3. It is a way of working. Besides the general modes of working characteristic of many Christians such as visiting the sick, doing personal work, helping the poor and keeping ourselves unspotted from the world, we must constantly work to keep sin out of our lives and out of the church. We must never cease to work against formalism, ritualism and liberalism on one hand and "antism," fanaticism and legalism on the other hand, for between these extremes is the way of holiness that leads to life.

4. It is a way of living. By their fruits of godliness and charity the early Christians were known. This way is a way of holiness not of mere separateness, but of consecration; a way of laying all possessions or attainments on God's altar, and a way of using all powers and opportunities for God's service.

THE GREAT WHITE THRONE

This sermon delivered at the Municipal Theatre
in the Gulf Coast Campaign for Christ,
1965, Mobile, Alabama.

Several years ago I was on my way to a meeting in Waukegan, Illinois. I had to change trains in Chicago, and as I stepped off the train and walked toward the station I saw literally hundreds of people. There were wives embracing their husbands, mothers embracing their children; all in a state of great happiness. No doubt some had been away from each other for weeks, some months, and possibly some even years. But as I continued to walk toward the station, I saw a small group standing together. Sorrow was written on their faces. And just about the time I got even with them, I heard a mother cry out, "That is my son that they are taking off the train now." When I heard those words I turned and they were taking a box off the train, loading it into a hearse. I said to myself, the judgment possibly will be something like this. There will be a great crowd, and to some it will be the happiest day and the happiest occasion they have ever known. To some it will be the saddest day they have ever known. There is no doubt in my mind but that mothers will be united with their children. There will be mothers separated from their children for eternity. I believe that the judgment is a real thing. I believe that we will all retain our identities. And, oh, what a happy occasion that will be for people to see their loved ones! But then on the other hand, this judgment day will be the saddest occasion that some people have ever known. And, oh, what a sad day it will be for those who lived and sinned away the day of grace. What an awful thing it would be to have to go to the judgment unprepared to meet God after being present on this occasion tonight and having every opportunity in the world to render obedience unto Christ.

In the book of Revelation, John was permitted to see things that no other person ever saw. It is interesting to read the book of Revelation and hear John tell about the things he saw. For instance, on one occasion he said he saw a white horse and a rider thereon. And John said he was going forth conquering and to conquer. On another occasion John said he saw a red horse and a rider, and he had a sword in his hand. He was going forth to take peace from the face of the earth. On another occasion John said he saw a black horse and its rider thereon. And he said he had a pair of balancing scales in his hands. Then again John said he saw a pale horse and its rider and his name was Death. And death and hell followed in his path. Then he said he saw souls that had been slain beneath the altar who had been slain for the word of God. But no doubt, the most startling thing that John ever saw while on the Isle of Patmos is recorded in Revelation 6:12-17 where John said,

> And I beheld when he had opened the sixth seal, and, lo, there was a great earthquake; and the sun became black as sackcloth of hair, and the moon became as blood; And the stars of heaven fell unto the earth, even as a fig tree casteth her untimely figs, when shaken of a mighty wind. And the heaven departed as a scroll when it is rolled together; and every mountain and island were moved out of their place. And the kings of the earth, and the great men, and the rich men, and the chief captains, and the mighty men, and every bondman, and every free man, hid themselves in the dens and in the rocks of the mountains and said to the mountains and rocks, Fall on us, and hide us from the face of him that sitteth on the throne, and from the wrath of the Lamb: For the great day of his wrath is come; and who shall be able to stand?

In Revelation 20:12 John said,

> And I saw the dead, small and great, stand before God; and the books were opened: and another book was opened, which is the book of life; and the dead were judged out of those things which were written in the books, according to their works. And the sea gave up the dead which were in it; and death and hell delivered up the dead which were in them: and they were judged every man according to their works.

No man can read these verses without his blood running cold. You just think of this scene that John saw. He said he saw that great white throne. What a scene that must have been. He said he actually saw the one who sat there; and he said that he was so great that the heavens fled from his presence because there was no place for them. Then he said, "I saw the sea give up all the dead that were in it. I saw death and hell deliver up the dead that were in them. And then I saw all these people go before that great white throne. I saw them stand there before the judge." One day you and I are going to stand before the throne that John saw. I ask you, in view of the fact that you are going to stand before that great white throne, in view of the fact that you are going to stand before this judge, are your books balanced tonight? What would you do if you knew that this night you were going to stand there? You may not stand there within the next few hours, but as surely as we are here you are going to stand there. It will not be long, because it will not be many days until this life will be over.

The Great Crowd

There may be many reasons why John referred to this as the "great throne". No doubt one reason was because of the crowd that he saw there. Have you ever thought of the crowd that will assemble around this throne? In Matthew 25:31-33 we are told:

> When the Son of man shall come in his glory, and all the holy angels with him, then shall he sit upon the throne of his glory: And before him shall be gathered all nations: and he shall separate them one from another, as a shepherd divideth his sheep from the goats: And he shall set the sheep on his right hand, but the goats on the left.

Adam and Eve will be present. Cain and Abel will be there. All the people who have lived in all ages of the world will be there. All those people who lived during the patriarchal dispensation will be standing before the great white throne when you and I stand there. All of these who lived during the Jewish age will be there. The ante-diluvians, post-diluvians, Asiatic peoples, Caucasians, Africans, Indians, every race, every tribe and every nation, all the Shemites, Hamites, and Jephethites, and rich and the poor, the wise and the unwise, those who have lived where they have heard about Christ, and those who have lived where they have never heard about Jesus Christ will all be there. Abraham will come from his cave of Machpelah and stand there with you and with me on that awful day of judgment. Moses will come from his unmarked grave in the land of Moab and stand before the throne with us. The Hadean world will open her mouth and all will stand before the throne to be judged of their deeds. Oh, what an audience that will be!

As I stand on this occasion and look out over the audience, I think of it as being a great audience. Can you, in your imagination, conceive of an audience where every person will be present from the time of Adam until time shall be no more? That is what John actually saw. He saw all the people standing there that had ever lived or ever would live. What an impression that made upon him, and what an impression it would make upon us if we would think seriously about that occasion.

The Open Books

The occasion is called the great day of judgment because of the books that will be opened. I do not know how many books will be opened on the day of judgment. I only know there is going to be a plurality of books, because John referred to them as "books". I know, for instance, that there is going to be a book of deeds. It is interesting in studying the Bible to observe that books are so often connected with the judgment. For instance, Moses said in praying to God that these people had committed a terrible sin and he said, "Oh, this people have sinned a great sin, and have made them gods of gold. Yet now, if thou wilt forgive their sin—if not, blot me, I pray thee, out of thy book which thou has written" (Exodus 32:32-33). Daniel said that he saw ten thousands times ten thousand stand before God. He said that the judgment was set and the books were opened. In Malachi 3:16, we are told that they who feared the Lord spoke one to another and the Lord heard them and their names were recorded in the book of remembrance. In Luke 10:20 when the disciples were rejoicing that spirits were subject to them, Jesus Christ said, "Rejoice not because spirits are subject to you, but because your names are written in the Lamb's book of life." In II Corinthians 5:10 Paul said, "We must all stand before the judgment seat of Christ to give an account of the things that we have done in our body according to that which we have done, whether it be good or bad."

The Recorded Book of Deeds

Thus I know the Bible teaches that the things we do in this life are recorded; and that just as surely as an individual dies having never repented of those sins, on the day of judgment, this book of deeds will be opened and there will be flashed before this individual every sinful, every evil, every ugly thing that he ever did in his life. It is for this reason that a man needs to accept Christ and have his sins washed away in the blood of the Lamb. It is for this reason that an individual who has once been born into the kingdom of God, but has fallen by the wayside, needs to make a confession of those sins, lest on that awful day of judgment all the evil things this individual has done in his lifetime be there to face him. I repeat, unless you repent of your sins, every evil thing you ever did in this life will be held against you at the judgment.

The Open Bible

I also know that the Bible itself is going to be opened. In John 12:48 Jesus Christ said, "He that rejecteth me and receiveth not my words hath one that judgeth him, the words that I have spoken." Notice this! "The same shall judge him in the last day." So we are going to be judged by the things written in this book. You know, if I were going to stand an examination, and if someone were to give me the book and tell me that all the questions are going to be taken from this book (and if I wanted to, I could even talk with the author of this book), do you not think that I would be very foolish to refuse to study this book or refuse to talk to the one who wrote this book when so much depends on the passing of this examination? I would not only want to see the book; I would want to study the book! I would be vitally interested in that one particular book because all the questions are going to be taken from it. And if I had an opportunity to talk with the one who wrote the book, I would want to do that. What would you think if I studied just about every book under the sun except the one that contains the answer? This is about what the average man in religion is doing, he is reading and studying every religious book he can get except the Bible. Many of these preachers can tell you what these religious teachers in the 18th, 19th and 20th centuries said, but it seems that they do not know what the preachers in the first century said, such as Paul, Peter, James, and Jude.

I want to relate to you, my friends, on that awful day of judgment we are not going to be judged by the doctrines of men. We are not going to be judged by the creed books that have been written by man. We are not going to be judged by what religious teachers have written and recorded. We are not going to be judged by what pastors have told us. We are going to be judged by the word of God itself; and it is for this reason that we should be vitally interested in what the Bible teaches. When we stand before that great white throne, this book is going to be opened.

We are going to be judged by the things written in this book and this book teaches that the alien sinner must believe on Christ. On the day of judgment, you will have to face that. This book teaches that the alien sinner is to confess his faith in Christ. On the day of judgment you will have to face that. This book teaches that the alien sinner is to be baptized into Christ for the remission of sins; that is, buried with his Lord in baptism. And on the day of judgment you are going to have to face it. You may get through this life rejecting it. You may get through this life denying it. But on the day of judgment the book is going to be opened and you and I are going to be judged by the things written in this book. I know then that there are two books that are going to be opened: the book of deeds, and the Bible.

The Lamb's Book of Life

From the statement John made in Revelation 21:27 there is going to be another book opened. You listen to it: "And there shall in no wise enter into it anything that defileth, neither whatsoever worketh abomination, or maketh a lie: but they which are written in the Lamb's book of life." John says the only people who enter into heaven are those whose names are written in the Lamb's book of life. It does not matter how honest or sincere or devout or upright a man may be, if that individual's name is not recorded in the Lamb's book of life, John says that man will never enter into the kingdom of heaven. Listen to him: he says, "But they which are recorded in the Lamb's book of life."

Now let me ask you this in all seriousness. Do you believe that a man's name is recorded in the Lamb's book of life if he refuses to obey the gospel? This book teaches that the alien sinner must believe, repent, confess, and be baptized into Christ. Do you believe that his name is recorded in the Lamb's book of life when he refuses to do this? And John said, "I saw those people that entered into heaven." He first tells us who will not enter into heaven, then he tells us who will enter into heaven: "they whose names are recorded in the Lamb's book of life." So an individual must render obedience unto the gospel.

A person may be a good moral man. He may be honest; he may be sincere; he may pay his debts; but, that man must contact the blood of Christ. When he renders obedience to the gospel, his name is recorded in the Lamb's book of life. And John said these are the ones who will enter into heaven.

The Awful Separation

This is also called the great throne because of the separation that will take place at the great white throne. You know, the word "separation" is a sad word. It disturbs us to be separated from those we love—even for a few days or a few months. I have a son from whom I have been separated for seven months. It would disturb me very much if I knew that it would be another seven months before I could see him. We do not like to be separated from those whom we love. If we could prevent it we would never be separated from them. But, oh, have you ever thought about the separation that will take place around that great white throne? I recall a few years ago in Louisiana there was a young man working in a bank, and for some reason this man did not handle the money properly. He misused some money and he was brought before the judge, tried, and then sentenced. The judge said, "I sentence you to the penitentiary for one year and one day." The wife screamed out in the courtroom and said, "I cannot bear to be separated from him for a year and a day." But she was. Oh, separation is a sad thing.

But the separation that will take place at the great white throne of God will be the saddest thing that you have ever thought about in all of your life; because on that day there will be wives separated from their husbands forever and forever. It is on that day that mothers will never see their sons again. It is on that day that some who have known each other on earth will never see each other again. You just cannot think of anything sadder than being separated forever and forever. And if hell were no more than that, (and it is more than that) that would be a terrible thing.

There was a lady who was a member of the Lord's church. She was a faithful, devoted Christian. She tried every way she could to try to encourage her husband to obey the gospel. But for some reason he could not see the importance of it. He sinned away the day of grace, and then finally died. When her children took her by the arm and walked up to the casket where he was, she took her warm hand and rubbed across his cold forehead and said, "Good-bye, John", and then she whispered, "forever." And then she cried like her heart would break.

Can you think of anything sadder than being separated from God forever and forever? And the man who dies in rebellion to God, the source of all light, will be separated from him forever. He is separated from all the holy angels forever. He is separated from everything that is good and holy and right forever and forever. Oh, it is a great throne because of the separation that will take place there.

The Righteous Judgment

It is also called the great throne because of the righteous judgment that will take place on that occasion. You know, many times when discussing the Bible with people, they will ask you about a loved one or relative who has died. Just a few weeks ago an individual asked me about his wife who had died. Well, you know, we can always answer like this, that regardless of how an individual dies he will receive righteous judgment. Is that not what you want, righteous judgment? I am so thankful that on the day of judgment some man is not going to judge me. Oh, I am just sure in that case I would never get to go to heaven! I am just sure that there are those who would be unfair, those who would be prejudiced toward me. Those might refuse to give me credit for what I have done; therefore, I thank God that I do not have to stand before men.

And I am also thankful that I will not be that Judge; because there might be some to whom I would not give justice, due to ignorance, human weaknesses, or prejudice. I am so thankful to God that I am not going to be the judge. Even if I did my very best I could still err in my judgment.

There is in Alaska tonight a tombstone erected over the body of a dead dog. In the frontier days there was a man who went out to hunt. He always left his favorite dog to guard his little girl. One day when he returned from his hunting trip this dog came running out to meet him with blood dripping from his mouth. When the hunter saw this he became hysterical and cried out, "My God, my God! That dog has killed my baby." So he started running and calling the child's name. The child did not answer. The dog was following at his heels. He took his sword and killed the dog. He continued to run through the house calling for his child. When he reached the back room the child was safe in the arms of its mother. Then the mother told how the child, while playing, was attacked by a wolf, and how the dog fought courageously and killed the wolf. She then showed him the dead wolf. You can imagine the frustration experienced by this man because he had erred in his judgment concerning the dog; and, therefore, had killed it.

Oh, I am so thankful that on the day of judgment no man will judge me. I am so thankful that I will stand before the Lord Jesus Christ. In Acts 17:30-31 the writer says,

> And the time of this ignorance God winked at; but now commandeth all men everywhere to repent; because he hath appointed a day in which he will judge the world in righteousness by that man whom he hath ordained whereof he hath given assurance unto all men in that he hath raised him from the dead.

So the judgment that will be rendered on that occasion will be righteous judgment. The apostle Paul said, "There is laid up for me a crown of righteousness which the Lord", notice the expression, "the righteous judge will give to me at that day. And not to me only but to all those who love his appearing." So the judgment that will be rendered on that day will be righteous judgment. And since it is going to be righteous judgment, I ask you, my friends, how is it with your soul right now? Since you know that you are going to stand before this judge and you know there is going to be righteous judgment, is all well with your soul?

The Judge On The Throne

This is called the great throne because of the one who sat there. John saw the Lord Jesus Christ sitting there. Jesus Christ is your Savior. In I Timothy 2:5, Paul says, "There is one God and one mediator between God and man, the man Christ Jesus." Jesus stands with outstretched arms saying, "Come unto me all ye that labor and are heavy laden and I will give you rest. Take my yoke upon you and learn of me for I am meek and lowly in heart and ye shall find rest unto your souls, for my yoke is easy and my burden is light." Jesus wants to save you now, he will save you today. But just as surely as we are gathered here, on the day of judgment when Christ sits upon the throne, he will not be sitting there as the Savior of the world. He will lay aside his redemptive robe and take up his judicial robe. The books will then be opened and we will be judged by the things that are written in the books.

Several years ago, in the state of Texas, a young lawyer was crossing the street. At the same moment, a team of horses was running away and about to run over a small boy in the street. The young lawyer risked his life and saved the child. The people in the town talked about what a noble and courageous thing he did. Many, many years went by. This young lawyer became a judge. The child grew to manhood and became a criminal. He was convicted of the terrible crime of murder and was brought before the judge. After the jury convicted him, he stood before the judge and the judge asked the young man, "Do you have anything to say?" Oh, there will be millions of people talking like this on the day of judgment. In his trembling voice and with tears coursing down his face he said, "Your honor, I have been told all of my life that when I was just a little boy you risked your life to save me. I stand before you again; I ask you this day to have mercy upon me and save my life." And then the judge said, "Young man, when I rescued you years ago I was your savior, but today I am your judge. You will have to be judged in the light of the law." Oh, I state to you, my friend, that Jesus Christ is your Savior. But when you sin away the day of grace, you must stand before that great white throne facing Jesus as your judge. Are you ready for that day? Are you prepared for it?

The Final Verdict

This was called the great white throne because of the verdict that will be rendered there. You know, just about every day we read in the newspapers of some court verdict that has been appealed. Some individual has been sentenced and has appealed his case to a higher court. But, oh, my friends, for you and me there will be no higher court! We will stand before the judge of all judges, the king of all kings, the prince of peace, and the priest of the most high God. We cannot appeal our case on that day. What will that verdict be with you? I can tell you what it will be. If you obey the Son of God, that verdict will be, "Well done, thou good and faithful servant." If you disobey God, what an awful thing that will be.

In one of the great art galleries there are two pictures hanging side by side. In one picture there is a mother standing with a baby in her arms and one standing by her side. The grandmother is also standing there and the door is slightly ajar. You can look through the door and see the prisoner sitting there. Beneath the picture are these words? "Waiting for the verdict." On the other picture the mother and father are standing side by side, and he is holding the baby. In this picture they are smiling! Underneath is printed the simple, though powerful word, "Acquitted." Oh, my friends, we had better pray to God that we may conduct ourselves in such way that on that awful day of judgment we can hear the Son of God say, "Acquitted, all is well."

It is on that day that a line will be drawn, and that line is going to separate angels from devils, the righteous from the unrighteous; and the sad thing about it is that that line will go down through just about every family that has ever lived on the earth. On one side of the line there will be everyone that rejected God. There will be the murderers, thieves, whoremongers, rebellious people, stubborn people, prejudiced people, and those who refused to obey God. There will be ministers who were not true to their trust. There will be false teachers. They all will be standing there. And, oh, what a scene that will be. Tears will be coursing the faces of all of those people. There will be a daughter looking into the face of her mother, screaming and crying and asking, "Why did you bring me to this awful place of destruction? It is too late now. The sentence has been rendered. The doom has been sealed. Eternity is getting ready to set in. And the door will be locked and never opened. And, oh, my God, my God, why will you not do something?" You can imagine what it will be like. They will cry; they will pray; they will scream; and John says, they will actually run. They will cry for rocks to fall on them. They will pray for mountains to crumble and fall and crush them. They will say, "Hide us from the face of the one that is on the throne."

It is going to be an awful thing, my friend, for those who are on the left side of that line. Oh, you may not think seriously about this.

You may think that you are not afraid, but John said, "I saw how they acted. I saw what they did." He said, "I saw them when they tried to run from God. I heard them scream as they were running." They were going toward the mountains and John said they were crying for the mountains to fall on them. "Hide us, hide us from the face of the one that sits on the throne." Oh, you cannot imagine what it will be like to be on the left. There will be some cursing their fathers. There will be some praying and asking, "Father, why did you bring me here? Why did you sin away the day of grace? Why did you reject God? Why did you not encourage me? Why did you encourage me to sin against God?" And while these people are standing on the left, tears coursing their faces; while they are crying and screaming; while they are trying to run and get away from the presence of God and Him that sits on the great white throne, the judge will rise. He will unsheathe that sword and he will hold it out and the stars will stand back beneath him, because the judgment will be set out in space. On that day, if you should flatten this old earth, there would not be room for them to stand. So the judgment will be out in space. The Son rises, unsheaths his sword, looks out over that crowd and says, "Depart from me into everlasting fire prepared for the devil and his angels." How can any man reject Christ knowing that day is coming?

But then let us look on the right hand. There are those who have obeyed God; widows who have escaped from their widowhood; orphans who have now been released from the orphanage; maidens with flowers in their hair put there by the angels of God; mothers smiling as they look onto the face of their children. The Son of God looks toward that audience and he smiles and heaven reflects a smile. All angels gather around them and they smile. There is the sweet face of Mary smiling. There is Abraham; he is smiling. There is Job who once had a lot of trials, but he is smiling. They are all standing on the right side. And then the Son of God looks out over them and he says, "Well done my good and faithful servants, enter into the joys of heaven." My friends, those are the things that John saw. He saw that great white throne. There are hundreds in this audience tonight who ought to do something about your condition. We are going to sing a song of invitation now. We want all of you who are unprepared to meet God to walk down the aisle while we stand and sing. Will you not come while we stand and sing?

HAPPINESS

This Sermon preached at the Plateau
Church of Christ, 1970.

I want to talk to you on a subject which every person in the world is seeking and desiring, happiness. He may be educated or uneducated, he may be rich or poor, or he may be very intellectual or unintellectual; but there is one thing for which he is looking, and that is happiness. Even a child is born in the world with that desire. This is demonstrated by his reaching for this thing or grabbing for that thing. The child is looking for contentment.

Some have estimated that science has added twenty years to the span of man's life, but science has not taught us how to be happy. Had you ever thought of this? Of all of the discoveries, of all of the inventions, of all of the things that man has learned, he has never been able to discover anything scientifically whereby he could add happiness to his life.

Happiness does not come as a result of direct search for it. If it did, then all gamblers, bribe-takers, and drunkards would be the happiest people in the world, because they are definitely seeking happiness. Theirs, however, is a warped conception of how happiness or peace of mind may be gained. For instance, the assertion in the Declaration of Independence says that all men have a right to the "pursuit of happiness." But actually, for an individual to be happy, he does not go around seeking happiness like you would chase a butterfly. When you see a butterfly fluttering around, you may run out and try to grab it. That is not the way an individual finds happiness. Happiness is not something that we seek as such. It is something that comes into our lives indirectly because of deeds that we have performed.

If you search for happiness
In a selfish sort of way,
Thinking only of yourself
And your own work or play
Happiness will never come to you.

But if you are always good and kind
To everyone you meet,
Helping every way you can,
With head and hands and feet,
Happiness will find its way to you.
                    Anonymous

Have you ever wondered why many rich people are not happy? Have you ever wondered why sometimes the wisest people in the world are not happy? Observe the news reports; who is it that kills himself? Who is it that takes an over-dose of sleeping pills? Many times it is the person that has everything the world can offer! Sometimes this person has beauty, glamour, wealth, and popularity; yet does not desire to live. Obviously, this individual had a warped conception of what happiness is and how one may have it. Nathaniel Hawthorne said, "Happiness in this world, comes incidentally." If one goes out pursuing happiness as such, he goes on a wild goose chase. W. D. Hoard said, "Happiness comes not from without but from within. It comes not from power of possession but from the power of appreciation."

William Lyon Phelps said, "Happiness is much more dependent on the mental attitude than on the external resources. This would be an absurdly obvious platitude, were it not for the fact that ninety-nine out of a hundred persons do not believe it." Charles C. H. Colton said, "There is this difference between happiness and wisdom: He that thinks himself the happiest man, really is so; but he that thinks himself the wisest, is generally the greatest fool." Make it your business to be happy and you are bound to be happy in your business. Much happiness is overlooked because it does not cost anything. Happiness is where it is found, and seldom where it is sought. Someone has said that happiness comes not from without but from within. It comes not from the power of possession but from the power of appreciation.

Happiness Comes From Helping Others

Many years ago there was a family that lived in Japan. They were known throughout the community as the happiest family that had been known. From family diaries that have been kept by the father and the grandfather and the great-grandfather, it was learned that for nine generations they were the happiest people in Japan. The fame of this outstanding family reached the emperor of Japan; whereupon, he sent one of his men to visit them and to have the patriarch write on a scroll the secret of happiness. In compliance with the emperor's request he sat down and carefully and slowly wrote until he filled the long scroll. Then the scroll was rolled up, carefully tied, and sent back to the emperor. He unrolled the scroll and this is what it said: "We find our happiness in doing good deeds for other people. We find our happiness in doing good deeds for other people." He had written the sentence repeatedly until he had filled the scroll. They had a true conception of happiness. Happiness came to them as a result of doing something for somebody else. Who is the happiest of men; he who concerns himself with the needs of others.

Happiness comes to all in service to others. For instance, when a child is fretted, a mother pacifies it. But when the child is contented, the mother is contented. The child is happy, the mother is happy. But the happiness came to the mother because she was doing something for somebody else. And that is the kind of happiness that is revealed in the Bible. Really, the only genuinely happy people in the world are people who spend their lives trying to do something for somebody else, making other people more faithful people.

A Texas millionaire once said, "I thought that money could buy everything, but I was miserably disillusioned." A movie star once said, "I have money, I have beauty, I have glamour, but I am miserable." A rich man once said, "I have lost all desire to live, yet I have everything to live for." A certain man went to a psychiatrist. He said, "I must have help. I am miserable, ill, tormented, wretched; I cannot live like this much longer, I must have help." The psychiatrist talked to him for a good while, then concluded, "I want you to do something for me, something that will help you. There is a circus in town. I went there last night and I saw a clown that was the happiest person I have ever seen in my life. He was so funny he would just die laughing and then because of his enthusiastic way of laughing everybody else was laughing. I want you to go tonight and see that clown, see how a man can live, see how a man can get joy out of living." And this person said to the psychiatrist, "I am the clown that you saw last night. That was just a front that I was putting on. Inside I am miserable while I put on this front because I get paid for doing it."

How many of us, in attempting to live the Christian life, put on a front of being happy, or being contented, of having peace of mind, when in reality we are miserable and wretched? Real happiness is not something that leaps up in one exilarating flash, and then sinks to a waning spark. The happiness that the Bible speaks of is happiness that is permanent in nature, it is real, it is genuine. But one may ask, "Now, Brother Black, you have presented the ideal. Why there are people in the world who would give millions of dollars to have this happiness that you are talking about, but how can an individual have this peace of mind? How can he have this genuine happiness?"

Let me ask you this: Do you believe that God intends for man to be miserable? Do you believe that God intends for his children to live wretched lives in this world? Certainly not. Oh, I am sure you would say, "No, God wants everybody to be happy." But the question is, "How is happiness to be sought?"

Happiness Is Found In Humility

Meekness is a quality which relates largely to men; and it means first that the man is humble. He bears himself among his fellowmen, not as a Caesar who, as Shakespeare says, doth "bestride the narrow world like a Colossus, beneath whose huge legs ordinary men may walk, and peep about to find themselves dishonourable men;" but he knows that he is only a man, and that the best of men are but men at the best, and he does not even claim to be one of the best of men. He considers himself to be "less than the least of all saints;" and, in some respects, the very "chief of sinners." Therefore he does not expect to have the first place in the synagogue, nor the highest seat at the feast; but he is quite satisfied if he may pass among his fellowmen as an humble Christian, and may be known by them as one who is a great debtor to the loving kindness of the Lord. He does not set himself up to be a very superior being. If he is of high birth, he does not boast of it; if he is of low birth, he does not try to put himself on a level with those who are in a higher rank of life. He is not one who boasts of his wealth, or of his talents; he knows that a man is not judged of God by any of these things; and if the Lord is pleased to give him much grace, and to make him very useful in His service, he only feels that he owes the more to his Master, and is the more responsible to Him. So he lies the lower before God, and walks the more humbly among men.

The meek-spirited man is always of humble temper and carriage. He is the very opposite of the proud man who, you feel, must be a person of consequence, at any rate to himself; and to whom you know that you must give way, unless you would have an altercation with him. He is a gentleman who expects always to have his topgallants flying in all weathers, he must ever have his banner borne in front of him, and everybody else must pay respect to him. The great "I" stands conspicuous in him at all times. He lives in the first house in the street, in the best room, in the front parlor; and when he wakes in the morning, he shakes hands with himself, and congratulates himself upon being such a fine fellow that he is! This is the very opposite of being meek. Therefore, humility, although not all that there is in meekness, is one of its chief characteristics.

Out of this grows gentleness of spirit. The man is gentle; he does not speak harshly; his tones are not harsh, his spirit is not domineering. He will often give up what he thinks to be good for himself, because he does not think it is expedient for the good of others. He seeks to be a true brother among his brethren; a doorkeeper at the house of the Lord, and a performer of menial services for the household of faith. I know some professing Christians who are very harsh and repellent. You would not think of going to tell them your troubles; you could not open your heart to them. They do not seem to be able to come down to your level. They are up on a mountain, and they speak down to you as a poor creature far below them. This is not the true Christian spirit; this is not being meek. The Christian who is really superior to others among whom he moves is just the man who lowers himself to the level of the lowest for the general good of all. He imitates his Master, who, though He was equal with God, "made Himself of no reputation, and took upon Him the form of a servant." And in consequence, he is loved and trusted as his Master was, and even little children come to him, and he does not repel them. He is gentle towards them, even as a loving mother who avoids all harshness in dealing with her children.

Happiness Results From Knowing God

We must recognize that real happiness comes as a result of knowing God as our Father. I am aware of the fact that there is a false impression in the world about the Fatherhood of God. Some teach that God is the father of everybody. I know this is true in the sense that God created the heavens and the earth. However, in John 8:44, Jesus asserted to some, "Ye are of your father, the devil." Jesus Christ did not seem to think that God was the father of everybody. He said, "Your father is the devil." But it is a wonderful feeling and a wonderful experience to know that God is our father.

God is the father of those who have been born into his family, just as you are the father of those who have been born into your family. When we properly understand this relationship we see ourselves as the richest people in all the world. This is one of the things that makes us happy as Christians—God is our father.

Furthermore, our father is rich. It was said that old Brother Harding, an eminent evangelist around the turn of the century, was once in a store in Nashville, Tennessee, to buy a suit of clothes. The salesman said to him, "Brother Harding, we always give preachers a discount. We feel like they need it because they are poor people." Brother Harding looked him straight in the eye and said, "What do you mean that preachers are poor people? I am one of the richest men in the world. My father owns the universe. My father owns the world. My father owns everything. I am a child of God. Indeed I am one of the richest men in Nashville." Brother Harding fully understood what it meant to be a child of God and he realized the true riches that came with it, peace of mind, contentment, and security.

A very poor Christian lady was once inviting another one to attend church services with her. The invited lady said, "I hesitate to go there to worship. Those people dress too nice. They are rich." "Yes, you are right, we do have many rich people down there and, thank God, I am one of the richest ones that go there to worship." She understood what it means to be a child of God. She understood genuine values. Is this the way you feel about being a child of God? I am one of the world's richest ones, because God is my father. He owns everything. There is no man in the world who can be genuinely and truly happy until he recognizes God as his Father.

Happiness Comes From Knowing
Christ As Our Saviour

Another step to this happiness that the Bible talks about is to know that Jesus Christ is our Saviour. In Revelation 1:5 John speaks of "Jesus Christ, who is the faithful witness, and the first begotten of the dead, and the prince of the kings of the earth. Unto him that loved us, and washed us from our sins in his own blood."

A missionary was once talking to a group of heathens. He told them the story of Christ; what Christ had done, what Christ meant to them, and how Christ had purchased the church with his blood. After he finished his speech he asked, "Do you people know now what I am talking about? Do you understand what it means when I say that Christ died for the sins of the world?" And one man stood up and said, "Yes, I understand it; it means that Jesus Christ took my place on the cross." I have an idea that these heathens had a better conception than some of us have of what is meant by the death of Jesus Christ. It actually means that Jesus Christ died on Calvary's cross, when I should have died on the cross. In I John 3:5, John said,

> He was manifested to take away our sins, but in Him there was no sin. I John 2:2, He is the propitiation for our sins, and not for ours only, but also for the sins of the whole world. I John 4:10, Herein is love, not that we loved God, but that he loved us, and sent his son to be the propitiation for our sins.

I will promptly confess to you that I do not understand all about the blood of Christ and its relationship to our sin, anymore than I understand why the blood of an animal could be put over the door in the land of Egypt and the firstborn in that house would not die. I do not understand how one can go down into that watery grave a sinner and come up out of that watery grave a saint. Yet I know the Bible teaches this. I know that God's Bible is the truth even though I do not understand how all of these things take place. I am like the man in John 9:25 who, in essence, said, "There are some things I do not know, but there is one thing I do know, I know that I was blind, but now I can see." Well, I know that I was once a child of the devil and now I am a child of God. And I know that this is a step toward true happiness.

Happiness Comes From Knowing
Our Sins Are Forgiven

Another step to true happiness is the knowledge that our sins are forgiven. You just think of the burden of being conscious of the fact that every sin that you ever committed is still held against you! Every evil thought you ever had and every bad deed you ever did is recorded in the book of deeds and held against you. No wonder people take sleeping pills. No wonder some jump out of windows. No wonder some shoot themselves. That burden is enough to cause a man to lose all desire to live. True happiness is found when we know our sins have been forgiven. In Revelation 1:5 we read,

> And from Jesus Christ, who is the faithful witness, and the first begotten of the dead, and the prince of the kings of the earth. Unto him that loved us, and washed us from our sins in his own blood. Acts 22:16 says, And now why tarriest thou? arise, and be baptized, and wash away thy sins, calling on the name of the Lord.

Not only have our sins been forgiven, but we are continually cleansed by the blood of Jesus Christ. In I John 1:7, John said, "If we walk in the light as he is in the light we have fellowship one with another and the blood of Jesus Christ his son cleanses us from all sin." This is the reason a child of God can lie on his pillow at night without worrying about what tomorrow holds. He knows **who** holds tomorrow. And if something should happen, he has the assurance that his sins are forgiven by the blood of Jesus Christ. Such assurance brings peace of mind to the person who is a member of the Lord's church.

Happiness is A Product of Prayer

Another step to happiness is the privilege of prayer. Had you ever thought what a terrible condition you would be in if all communication with God were cut? In James 5:16, James says, " . . .The effectual fervent prayer of a righteous man availeth much."

All the teachers at Freed-Hardeman College were wonderful people, but one man was my favorite, when I was there. A few years after I left school I learned that he had cancer. I was told the following concerning his sickness: When he went to the doctor he was a picture of health but they ran tests and learned that he was eaten up with cancer. He did not expect this. When he was told he had cancer in an advanced stage, he went to pieces. He went home and went into his room. His wife said he stayed in his room about two hours. As she would pass by she would hear him praying. She said when he came out of the room he was composed and did not seem to be disturbed about his condition even though he knew he must soon die. He never dreaded death. This, my friends, is what prayer means to the Christian. Christians find real happiness because of this privilege of prayer, being able to take their troubles to God through Jesus. You remember when they beheaded John the Baptist, the Bible says, in Matthew 14:10-12,

> And Herod sent, and beheaded John in the prison. And his head was brought in a charger, and given to the damsel: and she brought it to her mother. And his disciples came, and took up the body, and buried it, and went and told Jesus.

In most instances we tell everybody except Jesus Christ all about our trouble. The great song should mean much to us, notice what it says.

> I must tell Jesus all of my trials
> I cannot bear these burdens alone;
> In my distress He kindly will help me;
> He ever loves and cares for His own.
>
> I must tell Jesus all of my troubles;
> He is a kind, compassionate Friend;
> If I but ask Him, He will deliver,
> Make of my troubles quickly and end.
>
> O how the world to evil allures me!
> O how my heart is tempted to sin!
> I must tell Jesus, and He will help me
> Over the world the vict'ry to win.

Happiness Is Found In Service

Furthermore, one finds happiness in service. The happiest people living in the church today are the people who spend their lives actively engaged in the work of the Lord. When you talk to people who are not faithful, they will tell you that they have lost interest. Naturally the unfaithful lose interest, and they lose the joy, the peace, and the happiness that we are talking about. They lose this happiness because they stop doing things for other people. The happiest people in the world are the people who are working fervently in the kingdom of God, putting the kingdom of God first, not letting the things of this world drive Christ out of their lives. Real happiness consists in activity. Such is the constitution of our nature; it is a running stream, not a stagnant pool. If I were to suggest a general rule for happiness, I would say work a little harder; work a little longer; work!

Many people have happy homes and happy families. They are happy in their communities; they have a good influence on others; they maintain the respect of all decent and worthy citizens, and they even have special opportunities to lead others to Christ because they are really happy people. If you have not been putting the kingdom of God first in your life, you are not genuinely happy, and cannot be. Real happiness is cheap enough, yet how dearly we pay for it's counterfeit. In the close of my lesson I want to give twelve rules for happiness:

1. **Live a simple life.** Be temperate in your habits. Avoid selfseeking and selfishness. Make simplicity the keynote of your daily plans . . .Simple things are best.

2. **Spend less than you earn.** This may be difficult but it pays big dividends. Keep out of debt. Cultivate frugality, prudence and self denial. Avoid extravagance.

3. **Think constructively.** Train yourself to think clearly and accurately. Store your mind with useful thoughts. Stand porter at the door of your mind.

4. **Cultivate a yielding disposition.** Resist the common tendency to want everything your own way. Try to see the other person's point of view.

5. **Be grateful.** Begin the day with gratitude for your opportunities and blessings. Be glad for the privilege of life and work.

6.　**Rule your moods.** Cultivate a mental attitude of peace and goodwill.

7.　**Give generously.** There is no greater joy in life than to render happiness to others by means of intelligent giving.

8.　**Work with right motives.** The highest purpose of your life should be to grow in spiritual grace and power.

9.　**Be interested in others.** Divert your mind from selfcenteredness. In the degree that you give, serve, and help, you experience the by-product of happiness.

10.　**Live in the daylight compartment.** This means living one day at a time. Concentrate on your immediate task. Make the most of today for it is all that you have.

11.　**Have a Hobby.** Nature study, walking, gardening, music, golfing, carpentry, stamp collecting, sketching, voice culture, foreign language, books, photography, social service, public speaking, travel, authorship, are samples. Cultivate an avocation; to which you can turn for diversion and relaxation.

12.　**Keep close to God.** True and enduring happiness depends on close alliance with Him. It is your privilege to share His thoughts for your spiritual nourishment, and to have a constant assurance of Divine protection and guidance.

Before we sing the invitation I want to read to you Psalms the first chapter.

> Blessed (happy) is the man that walketh not in the counsel of the ungodly, nor standeth in the way of sinners, nor sitteth in the seat of the scornful. But his delight is in the law of the Lord; and in his law doth he meditate day and night. And he shall be like a tree planted by the rivers of water, that bringeth forth his fruit in his season; his leaf also shall not wither; and whatsoever he doeth shall prosper. The ungodly are not so; but are like the chaff which the wind driveth away. Therefore the ungodly shall not stand in the judgment, nor sinners in the congregation of the righteous: but the way of the ungodly shall perish.

Will you come to Jesus while we stand and sing?

PREJUDICE

This Lecture Delivered at Alabama Christian College,
Montgomery, Ala.

I read to you from I Timothy 5:21 where Paul in writing to Timothy said, "I charge thee before God, and the Lord Jesus Christ, and the elect angels, that thou observe these things, without preferring one before another, doing nothing by partiality." The word "prejudice" is not found in the King James version of the Bible, but the principle of prejudice is found throughout the Bible. The word prejudice means a prejudgment, rendering a decision without knowing all the facts in the case, making up one's mind with only partial information. When an individual does this, he is not being guided by reason or by knowledge, or by facts, or by Bible truth; instead he is being guided by prejudice.

It is a very unfortunate thing that most people are what they are religiously not because of a deep thorough investigation of the Word of God, but most people are what they are religiously because of tradition and because of prejudice. This is true in all religious bodies. No doubt there are those who are members of the church of Christ for no other reason, or at least they think they are members of the Lord's church. Certainly one should have scriptural motives in rendering obedience unto the gospel.

Will Rogers once said, "we are all ignorant, we are just ignorant about different things." And no doubt, all are prejudiced, but prejudiced about different things. Now I am sure that every individual present is prejudiced to some degree. I doubt if there is any individual living who is absolutely free of all prejudice. But no one should be so prejudiced that he would refuse to admit the truth when it is clearly shown what the truth is. Now this is the kind of prejudice that will damn the soul in hell. This is the kind of prejudice that will separate an individual from God.

Political Prejudice

All of us know there is much prejudice, for instance, in the political world. We have seen people who talk like this, "My father was a Democrat; my grandfather was a Democrat; my great grandfather was a Democrat; I am a Democrat. It would not make any difference who he is or what he stands for, I will vote the Democratic Ticket, even though I admit that the country would not prosper. Regardless of the man, I will vote this ticket." Now that is prejudice.

Sometimes we see individuals who reason after this fashion, if you can call it reasoning, "My father was a Republican, my grandfather was a Republican, and my great grandfather was a Republican, and regardless of what this Republican candidate stands for I will vote the Republican Ticket, and under no conditions will I vote the Democratic Ticket. And you could reason with me, you could show me ten thousand reasons why I should change, but I am prejudiced toward your party." Now that is prejudice.

There are many things wrong with our country, but one of the reasons this country is in the mess it is in is because countless millions of people go to the polls to vote without thinking about doing the **right** thing. Some do not pray over the matter; but they go vote a certain party ticket regardless of the consequences. And of course after awhile that would destroy any country. There is not a doubt in my mind but that this country is on the verge of destruction because millions of people are so prejudiced, politically that they cannot use reason and judgment when they go behind that curtain. And no man can tell you that this is not true unless he is so prejudiced that he could not see it. So those are prejudices, my friends, of the political world.

Because of our prejudice, people who are running for office, are often heard to say derogatory things about their political opponents, to poison the minds of the people. Had you ever wondered why those men do that? I can tell you why. If I can say something about an individual that will poison your mind, then you will not listen to him. Now that is the reason these men in their political speeches make these statements; they are trying to close your minds. In so doing, they are pretty shrewd because they know if they can ever close an individual's mind that there is no way in the world to reach that person. You know it is said that if an individual runs for some political office every mean, ugly thing that he has ever done in his life will be brought against him. Why? Because such information can close and prejudice the minds of people. It is used, therefore, as a weapon.

Prejudice is a terrible thing, yet very prevalent. Why, in time of war every nation uses propaganda to prejudice the minds of the people. You remember in World War II there was a woman in Germany who was referred to as Axis Sally. Do you know what her mission was during the war? It was to broadcast to the American boys that their wives back home were being untrue to them; that the American people did not appreciate what they were doing. Over and over and over, hour after hour, day after day, week after week, month after month she did that; and it was for the sole purpose of trying to poison the minds of these boys against our leaders. In the time of war, propaganda is used to prejudice minds.

I take for granted that no one present this evening is so guillible but he realizes many of our own commentators give out the news in such a way as to try to poison and to bias the minds of the people. They are often prejudiced, and they know the power of prejudice. A man who becomes prejudiced cannot be reasoned with. It is a terrible thing, my friends. Every man should pray to God, "Oh God, deliver me from this terrible disease of prejudice."

Social Prejudice

There is much prejudice in the racial world. I take for granted that no enlightened person would make the statement that there is no prejudice in the racial world. There is also much prejudice in the social world. For this reason sometimes we say that a certain individual came from the wrong side of the railroad track. What do people mean by that statement? It just simply means this: when he started out in life there was already one strike against him, or maybe two strikes against him, because of his community, his environment, or his surroundings. The people are prejudiced toward that particular class of people. This we call social prejudice.

Absalom and Prejudice

Now I have said all of that to say this: There is more religious prejudice in the world than there is political prejudice, social prejudice, or racial prejudice combined. There are many examples given to us in the Bible of people who were religiously prejudiced. I want you to observe some of these. For instance, in II Samuel the fifteenth chapter, we have an example that tells us about King David as he was reigning over God's people. Among his children, he had one son named Absalom, who wanted to reign over God's people. He wanted to sit on the throne. He was not in line for that position, but Absalom still had a desire to rule over God's people, to become king. He realized that he could not do it under ordinary circumstances, but Absalom was a shrewd young man, a very brilliant young man, and he came up with the idea, "if I can prejudice the minds of the people against my father, they no longer will listen to him. They will no longer take his advice, and if I so poison their minds that they will rise up in rebellion to my father, then there is a possibility that I can reign as king." So Absalom would go to the market place where the people would be talking about political matters—human nature has not changed very much. I can imagine the conversation would be going about like this. "You know, King David is taxing us to death. It seems that just about everything we make goes for taxes. David is described as being a just man, but he has not been running the affairs of government as he should."

Young Absalom would be there, and he would hear these words, and then he would join in and say, "Oh, if I were your judge. But, of course, you know I am not, but I can tell you one thing, if I were reigning over you there would be no trouble in all Israel. If I were reigning over you, you would not have these taxes. It would be a kingdom where everybody is happy, everybody loves his neighbor, lovers of peace." And then after making this speech, Absalom would embrace them and kiss them. The Bible says, "And so Absalom stole the hearts of all Israel." That just simply means that Absalom so poisoned the minds of those people that they would rise up in rebellion against his own father. And he continued to do this to the extent that he was able to raise an army and declare war on his own father. Then you tell me that prejudice is not a terrible thing, when some man can so prejudice and poison the minds of the people that they are in rebellion against the king and declare war on him!

Here is an example of the divine providence of God. There is a possibility that Absalom would have taken the throne of his father, but God, in his infinite wisdom saw to it that Absalom did not sit on that throne! He was killed while riding his beast in the wood of Ephram. God has given this example to let us see that prejudice is a terrible and dangerous thing.

Demetrius And Prejudice

And also in the New Testament, in Acts the nineteenth chapter, we find one of the most interesting examples that I have ever read. I want to tell you about the great gospel meeting that Paul was having in the city of Ephesus. He preached the gospel in such a way that when the people heard it, they rendered obedience unto it. We know they had truly repented, because in verse nineteen of the nineteenth chapter, "Many of them also which used curious arts, brought their books together, and burned them before all men: and they counted the price of them, and found it fifty thousand pieces of silver." Oh, that showed that they had truly repented. No doubt they were saying, "We never heard a man preach like this," and they were telling the truth. The apostle Paul was preaching the gospel, the death, the burial, the resurrection of the Lord Jesus Christ to these people, telling them that they could not be saved worshipping those false gods. He told them about the true God, and the people turned from their idols to the true God. Then they burned those books they had been reading to prove to the world that they had truly repented of their sins. Now would you not think that when a man like Paul came to town preaching the gospel and the people were repenting, everybody would be thrilled to death? Would you not say that you know that everybody is happy? Well, let us continue to read. In verse twenty-four of this same chapter it says, "A certain man named Demetrius, a silversmith, which made silver shrines for Diana with no small gain unto the craft." Now notice what he did. He called together the workmen of this occupation, and said, "Sirs, you know that by this craft we have our wealth." Now so far he has not said anything that I suppose he ought not to have said. He just called all the men together that worked with him, and he said, "You men realize that we have our work by making these little gods, do you not?" And I am sure they all answered in the affirmative, "That is right." But observe what he did, and said,

> Moreover ye see and hear, that not alone at Ephesus, but almost throughout all Asia, this Paul has persuaded and turned away much people saying that there be no gods, which are made with hands. So that now not only this our craft is in danger to be set at naught; but also that the temple of the great goddess of Diana should be despised, and her manificence should be destroyed, whom all Asia, and the world worshippeth. (Acts 19:25-27).

Now listen to this! "Now when they heard these sayings, they were full of wrath, and cried out saying, 'Great is Diana of the Ephesians.' " Great is this goddess that we have been worshipping.

Just a little while before, they said that we have never heard such a great preacher in our lives. We have never heard the gospel so explained in all of our lives. This is a great man of God; He was preaching the truth. But there was a certain man in town, whose business it was to poison and prejudice the minds of the people against the truth. Well, you might say, "Did not the apostle Paul say there were no gods made with hands?" Then you ask, "How can he poison the minds of the people?" He poisoned the minds of the people by telling them just part of the truth. A person who wants to prejudice the mind of another will always tell enough of the truth to get the confidence of the individual. I realize that it would be a strange doctrine today for one to talk to an individual and just start saying things in the very beginning that the individual knew to be untrue. He could not poison his mind. He must first get the individual's confidence and that is what Demetrius did. He called them together and said, "You men realize now that by this craft we have our wealth. This man, Paul, has come to town and has said that there are no gods made with hands." And there he stopped.

If he had told them all that Paul said, he would not have poisoned their minds. And speaking of those people he said, "This man, Paul, has come to town and he says there are no gods made with hands." He said, "This business in which we are engaged is not right and these little gods that we are making will not save the souls of anyone, but instead of putting your faith and confidence in these little gods, we should put our faith and confidence in the Lord Jesus Christ and that we should believe in God, and that the God who created the heavens and the earth is the God that is reigning in heaven. Therefore Paul is calling upon us to turn away from the gods that we are making and believe in the God that created the heavens and the earth." Truth does not poison the mind. He only told them enough of the truth to get their confidence. He said, "This man Paul has come to town and says there are no gods made with hands." But you know the implication of that, do you not? Listen to it, "This man Paul has come to town and he has destroyed our gods, and I just do not like to hear a man preach in such a way that he destroys our gods." Did you ever hear a person say, "That man comes to town and he just destroys; he tears down"? That is what Demetrius said about Paul. In other words, he left the inference that this man has come into town, he has taken away your gods, now you people do not have a god. What are you going to do?

When you take a person's god away from him, you disturb that individual. And when Demetrius made this speech—and it was a smooth speech—he just led them up to the point that, "Paul has come to town and he has destroyed your gods, and what are you people going to do about it? Are you going to stand for it? Are you going to let this man tell you that there are no gods made with hands? Are you people going to live without some god?"

When they heard what Demetrius said, they started crying, "Great is Diana of the Ephesians, great is Diana of the Ephesians!" No, he is not going to destroy our God. The same people just a short time before thought the apostle Paul was one of the greatest preachers that ever lived. Now these people are shouting, "Great is Diana of the Ephesians!" We are told that some of these people thought that Paul had gone into the theater, and the mob got so worked up and so disturbed that they raced into the theater thinking the apostle Paul was in there. And you know what the Bible says, in verse thirty-two? "Some therefore cried one thing and some another, for the assembly was confused and the greater part knew not wherefore they had come together." Is not that terrible? That just simply means that if you had walked into the theater and tapped one of those men on the shoulder and said, "Sir, my friend, what are you doing?", he would have said, "I am going to kill Paul if I ever get my hands on him." Well, now what has Paul done? The Bible says that over half of them would have said, "We do not know. We do not know what in the world he has done." What has he said? "We do not know what he said." What has he been teaching? "We do not know what he has been teaching." Well, what are you going to do? "We are going to kill the man."

My friends, prejudice is a terrible thing. Those people were so prejudiced that they rushed into the theater wanting to kill the apostle Paul, and the Bible says that the greater part of them did not even know what it was all about. Now that is sad. And it is sad to know that the very same thing is going on in the religious world today? Oh, Prejudice, my friends, is a terrible thing! Now this was recorded that we might read it, and that we might profit by it.

The High Priest And Prejudice

And then Acts the third chapter, if you remember, when Peter and John went up to the gate that is called Beautiful, they healed a man that had been lame from his mother's womb. He leaped for joy—he was healed. And when they asked what had taken place, the people were told that Peter and John had healed this man. I want to read to you how those people reacted, and I want you to keep in mind that these were religious people. You know, from the reading of this, unless we read the context, unless we explain what went on, why, somebody would get the idea that there was just a group of cut-throats in there. No! These were religious people. Some of them were the most religious people that ever lived. I want you to observe how they reacted to what Peter and John had done. When they called Peter and John in, they asked the question, "By what power and in whose name have you done this?" I do not know what they thought Peter and John would say, because they did not know Peter and John very well. You know, Peter was a very bold and courageous man, and I can see the court, men with robes and long beards down to their chests. They were sitting there in all dignity and splendor and they put these poor gospel preachers out there before them, and I can just see the chief spokesman. He says, "Now you tell us in whose name and by whose authority you made this man walk." And I can see Peter as he looks at them and he says to them, "Do you men remember the man that you men murdered a few days ago? You remember the one that you condemned to die on Calvary's cross because of your prejudice? Do you remember the one that taught those great truths which you despised to the extent that you killed him? Do you remember that man?" Peter said, "It was in his name that we made this man whole, in the name of the one that you killed."

Now, I want to read to you what the court decided. "When they saw the boldness of Peter and John and perceived that they were unlearned and ignorant men, they took knowledge of them that they had been with Jesus." Now listen to verse fourteen, "And beholding the man that was healed with them, they could say nothing against it." They said, "We would be foolish to deny it. There the man goes. You have seen him at the gate, have you not?" "Yes", someone says, "I have been seeing him there for over thirty years, but there the man goes leaping through the temple." So the court said, "We cannot deny this thing. We know that this thing is true."

Someone will say, "I can tell you what they did, Brother Black, they knew it was the truth." Well, what do you think they did? "Well", somebody says, "they called Peter and John in, and said, 'Men, we are sorry for what has happened. We want to apologize, because we falsely accused you men. Now there the man goes. We know that you men have done this thing and we want to extend to you the right hand of fellowship and bid you God's speed in this work that you are doing.' " No, that is not what they did!

I want to read to you. I am reading this to you so that you may see what prejudice will do. "But when they commanded them to go aside out of the council, they conferred among themselves." Now that was really—you talk about a conference—brother, here was a conference! And they said, "What in the world are we going to do with those men?" Now you listen to them as they talk, "We know that they are preaching the truth. Well, we would be fools to say that we did not heal this man, because there the man goes. Everybody knows the man. We know that these men are preaching the truth." But let me read it to you; "But that it spread no further among the people." What is it that they do not want to spread among the people? The truth—what these men have done.

Now somebody says, "Brother Black, do you think that people could be that prejudiced in religion?" Well, I just ask you, do you believe the Bible? That is all the comment I can make. That is what the Bible says. Those men knew that these men had performed this miracle, we know that it is the truth, we cannot deny it, but they had a conference and they said, "Men, what are we going to do? What decision can we make?" They said, "That it spread no further among the people, let us straitly threaten them." Do what? "Let us threaten them." Threaten them for what? "Well, we know that they are preaching the truth. We know it is right, but we cannot admit the truth. Our fathers and grandfathers would frown on them. We cannot admit that this is the truth. There is a lot of pride involved in this." So the first thing that they decided was this, "We cannot accept the truth!" But they said, "We have got to render some decision with these men. What are we going to say?" They said, "That it spread no further, let us threaten them." Now what? Threaten them! What was the threat? "That they speak henceforth to no man in this name. Let us tell them, do not even be guilty of preaching in this name again. Now men, we know what you did was the truth, we cannot deny it. What you said was the truth. But do not ever be guilty of saying it again."

Why do you suppose that God recorded that, my friends? I am telling you, we had better come to our senses. We had better lay aside this prejudice if we expect to go to heaven when we die. It is not a matter of being prejudiced toward some individual, it is just a matter of being prejudiced toward God's truth, and here is a clear-cut example of it, an example that shows what prejudice will do to people when their hearts are filled with it. They said, "We know that it is the truth, but we are not going to admit it, we are not going to obey it."

That was the decision they rendered, so I can just hear them as they talk, they no doubt say, "How are we going to break the news to those two men?" Well, somebody speaks up, "Bring them in the court. We will make this thing official." So they brought them in and commanded them—listen to this—and commanded them not to speak at all, you think of that, not to speak at all nor teach in the name of Jesus. Can you conceive of a person being that prejudiced? Can you conceive of a person becoming so prejudiced that he would say, "Do not ever be guilty of speaking in the name of the Lord Jesus Christ."

Well, this is interesting, and I am so glad that Peter said this. I am glad that Luke recorded what Peter said because, brother, this gives me courage. But Peter and John answered and said unto them, "Whether it be right in the sight of God to hearken unto you more than unto God, judge ye." Now you men are great judges, are you not? Now, here is something for you to judge! Now you just make up your mind whether you think we are going to obey you or whether we are going to obey God. And that is the way that Peter left it!

Now why do you suppose that that is recorded, my friends? I can tell you. That has been recorded to let us see the danger of prejudice. It is the most terrible thing in the world. And yet you know that the world is filled with it. Read Acts the fourth chapter.

Many individuals live, what he might refer to as a religious life, and still let their lives be governed by dark blind prejudice. We learn from the Bible what prejudice will do.

The Court And Prejudice

Even in this age there is much prejudice. You have heard the judge ask the future jurors, "Do you know anything about this case? Have you discussed it on the street? Have you been reading about it in the newspapers? Have you partially made up your mind?" You listen to the individual. He says, "Yes, your honor, I have discussed it on the job several times, I have been keeping up with it in the newspapers, and I listened to it on the newscast." Do you know what the judge says? "Then you are not qualified to serve on this jury." Why? Because the judge knows that if you have already partially made up your mind, even the judge knows that you cannot render a fair decision.

Now why is it that when we stand before people and preach the simple truths of God that many times these truths do not register? I can tell you, and I do not want to be ugly, but the reason these truths do not register many times is because the individual has already rendered a decision, and what the truth of God has to say has no bearing upon the person.

What Prejudice Will Do

Prejudice will even cause people to kill. In Acts the seventh chapter is one of the greatest speeches that ever fell from the lips of man. When Stephen delivered that speech the Bible says, "They rushed upon him," now you listen to it, "and they gnashed upon him with their teeth." Can you conceive of a group of grown men, rushing upon a man, knocking him down, and actually biting him? That is what prejudice will do! That is why they killed Stephen. They were so prejudiced toward the truths of God that when Stephen spoke, their hearts were filled with hate and malice and they said, "We will kill that man." Oh yes, prejudice will cause people to murder. It is a terrible thing.

Prejudice will cause people to close their eyes and stop their ears. That is the reason that people could not understand Jesus Christ. As he spoke these parables recorded in Matthew the thirteenth chapter and verse fifteen, Jesus Christ said,

> For this people's heart is waxed gross, and their ears are dull of hearing, and their eyes they have closed; lest at any time they should see with their eyes, and hear with their ears, and should understand with their heart, and should be converted, and I should heal them.

Those are some of the things that prejudice will do.

The Remedy For Prejudice

But someone may ask, "What is the remedy for prejudice?" It is found in John the first chapter, when Philip said to Nathaniel, "Come and see." It is also found in Acts the seventeenth chapter and verse eleven where Luke says, "The Bereans were more noble than those in Thessalonica in that they received the word with all readiness of mind and searched the scripture to see whether those things were so."

In II Timothy two and verse fifteen, "Study to shew thyself approved unto God, a workman that needeth not be ashamed, rightly dividing the word of truth." That is the remedy for prejudice. Why, if we had time, I could give you example after example of modern day prejudice. Why it has not been too long ago that I was talking to a lady about rendering obedience unto the gospel, and I took the Bible and turned to Acts the second chapter. I read with her what those people did on the day of Pentecost, how that Peter preached to them and they believed what Peter said and they repented of their sins and were baptized for the remission of sins. And that lady with tears running down her cheeks said this, "Brother Black, I know that that is what the Bible says," but she said, "You know I just cannot say my mother is in hell." And I had not said a word about her mother. Why did she get this idea? Who told her that? Who told her that if she obeyed the gospel, she had to be saying that somebody was in hell? I can tell you. Somebody told that lady that, for the sole purpose of poisoning her mind against God's eternal truth!

Examples Of Prejudice Today

How many times have I heard an individual say in talking to him about obeying the gospel, "You believe that nobody is going to heaven except you and your little group." How many times have you heard that? Why is that said? That is said for the purpose of poisoning the minds of the people. I never made a statement like that in my life. You never heard a gospel preacher make a statement like that if he knew what he was talking about. I do not even have a little group! You may have heard a preacher read from the word of God these verses,

> Ye who are troubled, rest with us when the Lord Jesus Christ shall descend from heaven with his angels in flaming fire, taking vengeance on them that know not God and obey not the gospel who shall be punished with everlasting destruction from the presence of the Lord and from the glory of his power.

Now you believe that, do you not? Surely you do, surely you believe that people must obey the gospel. But why are these things worded like that? I can tell you. For the purpose of poisoning the minds of the people.

I was talking to a lady once about obeying the gospel and you listen to this. She said, "Brother Black, there is no doubt in my mind but what the Bible teaches that a person must believe in Christ, repent of his sins, confess his faith in Christ, and be baptized into Christ for the remission of sins." She said, "I believe that with all my heart," but she said, "there is one thing that I cannot understand." I asked, "What is that?" She said, "I cannot understand why a person has to be baptized every time he sins." Well, I said, "I did not know that either, lady. It would be ridiculous, would it not?" In that case, a person would have to go, sometimes two or three or four times a day. No, I do not believe that. I do not know of any gospel preacher that believes that. But the thing that I am trying to impress upon your mind is, who told her that? Where did she get that information? Why did an individual say that? I can tell you why. That was said for the purpose of trying to poison her mind against what God said on the subject of baptism.

The Bible teaches that an individual is baptized into Christ, Galatians 3:27; that he is baptized for the remission of sins, Acts 2:38; that he is buried in baptism, Romans 6:4. Now that would not prejudice the mind, would it? But can you not see how statements can be made for the purpose of poisoning the mind of people, just like Demetrius did at Ephesus? But I can tell you something, my friends, we had better be careful. We had better be exceedingly careful, because it will not be long until we are going to stand on the day of judgment, and we are going to be judged by this book. Now as far as I know, an individual can get through this life by being prejudice, but you cannot get into heaven with it, because God despises it.

People Who Were Not Prejudiced

I have preached overtime but this is a great subject, and in the next two or three minutes I want to mention to you some people who were **not** prejudiced that you might have a greater appreciation for this lesson. In Acts the second chapter these Pentecostians were not prejudiced. Some of those people were there who crucified the Lord Jesus Christ, but when Peter stood before them and preached to them, they believed the truth, and they asked, "Men and brethren, what shall we do?" And Peter said, "Repent and be baptized every one of you in the name of Jesus Christ for the remission of sins and ye shall receive the gift of the Holy Spirit." In verse forty-one it says, "And they that gladly received the word were baptized, and there were added unto them that day about three thousand souls." Verse forty-seven says, "And the Lord added to the church daily such as should be saved." Now that is what happens when people are not prejudiced.

Let me give you another example. In Acts the eighth chapter, when the Ethiopian eunuch was returning from Jerusalem to his homeland, Philip met him and preached unto him Jesus. And the eunuch, after he heard Jesus, said, "See here is water, what doth hinder me from being baptized?" If he had been a prejudice man, he would have said, "No I am not going to be baptized. I am not going to obey that." And then he would have started making charges at the preacher.

In Acts the sixteenth chapter is another example. When Paul went to the river bank and preached to Lydia, the Bible says that her heart was opened, just as every man's heart is opened when he is not prejudiced. I can tell you one thing, my friend, and you put this down, when the Bible says that the Lord opened the heart of Lydia, that just simply means that she was not prejudiced, because the word of God never opens the heart of any man if he is prejudiced toward the truth. And on and on we could go with those who are not prejudiced.

So I ask you in the close of this lesson, honest before God of heaven, is it prejudice that is keeping you from rendering obedience unto the gospel? Is it prejudice that is keeping you outside the family of God? You need to ask yourself this question, my friends, because it will not be long—this life is not very long. At the most, we will be here for just a little while. Then we are going to stand before the great Judge. In John 12:48, Jesus said, "He that rejecteth me and receivest not my words, hath one that judgeth him, these words that I have spoken the same shall judge him in the last day."

How will it be with you, my friends? This life is too short for a man to be prejudiced. This life is too short for a man to close his eyes to the truth. You cannot afford to do it. I cannot afford to do it. We must be honest; we must be sincere; we must love the truth and we must want it. If you are here and you have never obeyed the gospel, I ask you, will you open your heart and let the Lord come in? While we sing the invitation, will you ask yourself, "Am I prejudiced? Do I have an open mind toward the truths of God?" While we stand and sing, will you come?

THE MEANING OF CHRISTIAN STEWARDSHIP

This Lecture Delivered At
Alabama Christian College, Montgomery, Ala.

INTRODUCTION

It is impossible for a Christian to be happy in rendering service to God without knowing the true meaning of Christian stewardship. What is a steward? Webster says of a steward, "An officer or employee in a large family, or on a large estate, to manage the domestic concerns, supervise servants, collect rents or income, keep accounts, etc., an administrator, or supervisor; a manager." We learn from this definition that a steward is one who takes care of material things that belong to someone else. It is impossible for one to be a faithful Christian unless he realizes that he is only a possessor and not the owner of material things.

The Christian has no option in the matter of being a steward. Everyone is a steward whether he wants to be or not, he may choose to be a bad one or a good one but he is still a steward. At the judgment the Lord will demand an account of the way we have used our time, talent, money and everything that God has entrusted to us. It does not matter how much or how little of this worlds goods we possess, we are going to give an account to God on that awful day of Judgment.

A CHRISTIAN STEWARD RECOGNIZES DIVINE OWNERSHIP

A Christian steward recognizes the fact that he is only a steward, and in reality he does not own anything. If one could convince himself that he owns no land, no money for the simple reason that God claims divine ownership to everything. In your mind picture a man working in a bank, and after a few months of employment he is able to convince himself that he owns the bank. One may ask, "How could one come to such a conclusion?" He could come to this conclusion by using the kind of reasoning that many members of the church use when they get into their mind the idea that they own the material things of this world and fail to recognize God as the owner.

Hear with what authority the Bible speaks along these lines: "Every good endowment and every perfect gift is from above, coming down from the Father of lights with whom there is no variation or shadow due to change." (James 1:17). Many of the early Christians recognized this: "Now the company of those who believed were of one heart and soul, and no one said that any of the things which he possessed was his own, but they had everything in common." (Acts 4:32). God's title to the whole universe and everything in it is clearly established in the Bible. "In the beginning God created the heavens and the earth." (Gen. 1:1). Not any one of us had anything to do with the creation. How strange it is to see one act as if he made the heavens and the earth. "The earth is the Lord's and the fulness thereof, the world and those who dwell therein." (Ps. 24:1). "The silver is mine, and the gold is mine, says the Lord of hosts." (Hag. 2:8). "For every beast of the forest is mine, the cattle on a thousand hills." (Ps. 50:10). "Behold, all souls are mine; the soul of the father as well as the soul of the son is mine; the soul that sins shall die." (Ezek. 18:4). "Do you not know that your body is a temple of the Holy Spirit within you, which you have from God? You are not your own; you were bought with a price. So glorify God in your body." (I Cor. 6:19,20). " . . .Fear not, for I have redeemed you." The reason the Macedonians were such liberal givers is because they had a true conception of Christian Stewardship. (Study 2 Cor. 8).

Steward I and not possessor of the wealth entrusted me.
What, were God himself the holder, would His disposition be?
This I ask myself each morning, every noon, and every night
As I view His gentle goodness with ever new delight.
—Strickland Gillien

A CHRISTIAN STEWARD HONORS GOD
WITH HIS FIRSTFRUITS

The faithful steward will pay to his landlord all that is due him. What would you think of a tenant who gathered his crop and instead of giving the landlord his share, he just brings him a sack of corn and says, "Thank you." It seems that many members of the church don't ever, as much as say, "Thank you" to God. "Honor the Lord with your substance and with the firstfruits of all your produce; then your barns will be filled with plenty, and your vats will be bursting with wine." (Prov. 3:9,10). It is interesting to observe that at the times when God's people were at a very low spiritual condition and when Israel was having her greatest spiritual decline and most severe material reverses, it was always when they did not give to God liberally. Listen to Malachi,

Will man rob God? Yet you are robbing me. But you say, "How are we robbing thee?" In your tithes and offerings. You are cursed with a curse, for you are robbing me; the whole nation of you. Bring the full tithes into the storehouse, and there may be food in my house; and thereby put me to the test, says the Lord of hosts, if I will not open the windows of heaven for you and pour down for you an overflowing blessing. (Mal. 3:8-10).

It is one of God's cardinal facts that when a steward gives to God off of the very top of his income that he is wonderfully blessed. Will you read and study carefully the following words?

I also found out that the portions of the Levites had not been given to them; so that the Levites and the singers, who did the work, had fled each of his field. So I remonstrated with the officials and said, "Why is the house of God forsaken?" And I gathered them together and set them in their stations. Then all Judah brought the tithe of the grain, wine, and oil into the storehouses. (Neh. 13:10-12).

Azariah the chief priest, who was of the house of Zedok, answered him, "Since they began to bring the contributions into the house of the Lord we have eaten and had enough and have plenty left; for the Lord blessed his people, so that we have this great store left." Then Hezekiah commanded them to prepare chambers in the house of the Lord; and they prepared them. (II Chron. 31:10-11).

It is possible for one to give abundance unto the Lord and yet be rejected. The Lord not only wants us to be liberal in our giving, but He wants the first and the best.

What a weariness this is, you say, and you snuff at me, says the Lord of hosts. You bring what has been taken by violence or is lame or sick, and this you bring as your offering! Shall I accept that from your hand? says the Lord. Cursed be the cheat who has a male in his flock, and vows it, and yet sacrifices the Lord what is blemished; for I am a great King, says the Lord of hosts, and my name is feared among the nations. (Mal. 1:13-14).

When Paul wrote to the church in Corinth he said: "Moreover it is required of stewards that they be found trustworthy." (I Cor. 4:2). We as faithful stewards are to use wisely everything that God has entrusted to our care. The steward that fails to use these things wisely will be condemned.

Then you ought to have invested my money with the bankers, and at my coming I should have received what was my own with interest.

So take the talent from him, and give it to him who has the ten talents. For to every one who has will more be given, and he will have abundance; but from him who has not, even what he has will be taken away. And cast the worthless servant into the outer darkness; there men will weep and gnash their teeth. (Matt. 25:27-30).

THE CHRISTIAN STEWARD KNOWS
HE MUST GIVE AN ACCOUNT

We must give an account of the way we make money and also the way we spend it. "For who sees anything different in you? What have you that you did not receive? If then you received it, why do you boast as if it were not a gift?" (I Cor. 4:7). Isn't it strange in the light of what Paul says that some act as if God had nothing to do with what they have in this world. Some act as if by their own power, ability and wisdom they have been able to accumulate much of the world. So often we hear one say, "My house, my land, my cattle, my bonds, my barns, my crop, my bank account, etc." When I hear one talk like this I always ask whose will these things be one hundred years from now? No, my friend, you do not own anything and you must learn this important lesson to be a good steward. The very fact that you cannot carry anything out of the world with you when you die is indicative of the fact that you don't own anything.

I heard of a man who loved money so dearly that he had all of it converted into gold so he could take it to heaven with him when he died. He said gold was good in any country. He put all of his gold up in the attic and told his family he would get it as his spirit went up through the attic. A few days after he died, one of the boys went up in the attic and observed that the gold was still there. He came down and said, to his mother, "Dad did not get that gold." She said, "I told him if he was going to take it with him he had better put it in the basement, then he could get it on the way to the place where he was going."

Every Christian needs to study carefully the following verses.

There is great gain in godliness with contentment; for we brought nothing into the world, and we cannot take anything out of the world; but if we have food and clothing, with these we shall be content. But those who desire to be rich fall into temptation, into a snare, into many senseless and hurtfull desires that plunge men into ruin and destruction. For the love of money is the root of all evils; it is through this craving that some have wandered away from the faith and pierced their hearts with many pangs.

As stewards we must give an account of our time. Life and time are given to us and we are to use them as his stewards. We do not create either. If we could realize how precious time is, we would be better stewards in dealing with it. "So teach us to number our days that we may get a heart of wisdom." (Ps. 90:12). We cannot do with time as we can with money. We cannot lay time up and use it for some future date. If we do not use time as it comes to us it is gone forever.

Time is as sacred as life itself. God has made every day of our lives precious with opportunities for speaking a kind word, lending a helping hand, doing some good deed, rendering some Christ-like service. The moments that are so golden, should be valued in the highest degree and used to promote the cause of Christ. The brevity and uncertainty of time, so far as we are personally concerned, give added emphasis to its preciousness and sacredness. The misuse and wasting of time is one of the most prevalent of the besetting sins of Christians.

Every steward must give an account of his influence. We cannot shut our lives away from men nor avoid the serious responsibility of the stewardship of our influence. We cannot go through life in isolation. What we say and do influences those around us. "None of us lives to himself, and none of us dies to himself." (Rom. 14:7). The fact that we are often unconscious of the influence we are exerting, only magnifies the seriousness of the fact. In the home, in business or in the church, the Christian is ever influencing others.

We are stewards of the gospel. The only feet the Lord has to carry the gospel to the world are our feet. A good steward loves the gospel and will do all in his power to see that others hear it. A good steward will try to please his master. We are pleasing the Lord when we are carrying his gospel to those who have never heard of Christ. Christian stewards are responsible for the perservation and spreading of the gospel. A faithful steward will never be happy in keeping the gospel at home.

WHO IS A GOOD STEWARD?

There is a three-fold duty of a good steward: 1. Make all he can. 2. Save all he can. 3. Give all he can. I heard of an old miser hearing a preacher discuss these three points. The preacher made his first point. "Make all you can." The old miser smiled and said, "Amen." The preacher said my second point is, "Save all you can." The old miser almost shouted and said, "I never heard a man who knows, so much, and who can tell it with such a pleasing personality." The preacher said my third point is, "Give all you can." The old miser fainted.

1. The Bible teaches that it is the duty of a good steward to make all he can. In Matthew, the 25th chapter, the five talent and the two talent men were commended because they made all they could. The one talent man was condemned because he did not make all he could have made. (Read Matthew 25:14-27). "Let the thief no longer steal, but rather let him labor, doing honest work with his hands, so that he may be able to give to those in need. " (Eph. 4:28). It is an honorable thing for a man to work and to make money, for God expects this of a good steward. There is not anything wrong with a man working and making all he has the ability to earn. God condemns slothfulness. "For even when we were with you, we gave you this command: If any one will not work, let him not eat." (II Thes. 3:10). "Never flag in zeal, be aglow with the Spirit, serve the Lord." (Rom. 12:11).

2. Save all you can. "And when they had eaten their fill, he told his disciples, Gather up the fragments left over, that nothing may be lost." (Jn. 6:12). Jesus used this occasion to impress upon the minds of his disciples that it is just as sinful to be wasteful as it is to hoard. God wants his children to be industrious and thrifty. I have observed that the thrifty people in the church are the ones who support 90% of the Lord's work. I am talking about a thrifty person, not a miser. "Here for the third time I am ready to come to you. And I will not be a burden, for I seek not what is yours but you; for children ought not to lay up for their parents, but parents for their children." (2 Cor. 12:14). It is not wrong for a man to make provisions for his family nor for the future.

3. Give all you can. "On the first day of every week, each of you is to put something aside and store it up, as he may prosper, so that contributions need not be made when I come." (I Cor. 16:2). Our giving is to be done as God has prospered us. If all members of the church were true to this trust we could evangelize the world in a short time. Why do you want a raise? For your own selfish pleasure or do you want it that you may be able to give more to the Lord's work. Why do you want to make more in your business; for self or to do good to others?

CHRIST THE HOPE OF THE WORLD

Lecture delivered at Freed-Hardeman College,
February, 1973, Henderson, Tenn.

INTRODUCTION

I Pet. 3:15, "But sanctify the Lord God in your hearts: and be ready always to give an answer to every man that asketh you a reason of the hope that is in you with meekness and fear." The exaltation of Christ to the priesthood after the order of Melchizedec offers to the Christian the only real and everlasting hope he has in this world and in the world to come. Heb. 7:19, "For the law made nothing perfect, but the bringing in of a better hope did; by the which we draw nigh unto God."

This hope that Jesus Christ offers is not diminished by tribulations, but on the contrary, is strengthened by it and is, accordingly termed a helmet. I Thes. 5:8, "But let us, who are of the day, be sober, putting on the breastplate of faith and love; and for an helmet, the hope of salvation."

The Christian hope, in all probability, is the strongest incentive to encourage the child of God to remain faithful in the face of heartache and tribulations. Seeing, therefore, that we have such solid ground to build upon, such a full assurance of faith, we may cast the anchor of our hope on God's eternal shore and walk through the Valley of Death fearing no evil. It was upon this doctrine of hope that Christ taught the greatest lessons known to man. By it Jesus taught his disciples to be patient in tribulations, to suffer cruel persecution because of this hope that Jesus Christ offered. Through protracted sickness and a thousand temptations they proved their fidelity to God, sustained by this glorious hope.

When the enemies of Christianity would take the apostle Paul and beat him across his back until his shoulder blades looked like white caps in a sea of blood, and with every lick the muscles tighten, the flesh quivers, the blood flows, and yet this great man carried on his preaching. Why? He was sustained by the glorious hope that Jesus Christ offered. How could those early Christians march into the arena facing the blood thirsty lions? They knew they had obeyed Jesus and they knew that Jesus Christ was the hope of the world. When one of the early Christians was being burned to the stake, he said to the tormentor just before he set fire to him, "Feel of my pulse and see if it is not calmer than yours." When his fingers lighted up like candles he prayed for his tormentors. Why? Because he knew that Jesus Christ was and is the hope of the world.

A real and genuine hope cannot be found in the scientific discoveries of man. Our hope is not in the Summit meetings of the leaders of the powerful nations of the world. Our hope is not in the discovery of facts we may learn by going to the moon or learning if there is life on Mars. Our hope is not in nuclear powers. Our hope is not in becoming a mighty and powerful nation that might destroy the weak and unfortunate. Our hope is not in scientific facts, knowledge of medicine, education, philosophy, phenomenology nor the wisdom of man. Our hope is in Jesus Christ who is the Prince of peace and Priest of the most High God.

JESUS IS OUR HOPE BECAUSE HE IS
THE SON OF GOD

The Old Testament scriptures foretold the coming of Jesus Christ. While Jesus was carring on his public ministry he endorsed the prophets and prophecies as being inspired of God. Our Lord filled his sermons with quotations from the Old Testament. Matthew, Mark, Luke and John all quote from the Old Testament. Jesus and his apostles believed the Old Testament to be the inspired word of God.

One of the Old Testament characters that lived seven hundred years before Christ said,

> Isa. 9:6: For unto us a child is born, unto us a son is given; and the government shall be upon his shoulder: and his name shall be called Wonderful, Counsellor, The mighty God, the everlasting Father, the Prince of Peace.

When Matthew speaks of the birth of Christ he quotes from the Old Testament, Matt. 1:22-23:

> How all this was done, that it might be fulfilled which was spoken of the Lord by the prophet, saying, Behold, a virgin shall be with child, and shall bring forth a son, and they shall call his name Emmanuel, which being interpreted is, God with us.

John the Baptist referred to Jesus Christ after this order: Jn. 1:29, "The next day John seeth Jesus coming unto him, and saith, Behold the Lamb of God which taketh away the sin of the world."

The hope of the human family centers in and cluster around Jesus of Nazareth. He is the only physician that has shown himself able to heal the soul's deepest maladies. He is the only one that has a heart large enough to take in the whole human family. Some have been able to love a few individuals; we call them benevolent men. Some have been able to love certain classes; we call them philanthropist. Some have been able to love a nation; we call them patriots. But Jesus of Nazareth is the only one whose philanthropy overleaped all barriers of race or class or nationality and embraced all men irrespective of any adventitious or ennobling circumstances. He is the only one who has a purpose great enough to include the whole human family.

All philosophers with their imperfect teachings, have faded away and are almost forgotten; but his teachings command the attention of the learned and the ignorant, the great and the small. The church has succeeded and will continue to succeed because we have Christ leading us to a victory.

The Jews had their Moses, Rome had her Caesar, France had her Napoleon, England had her Gladstone, America had her Washington, but thanks be to God the church has Jesus Christ as the captain of our salvation. If it were possible for George Washington, the Father of our country, to walk into our midst we would rise to our feet; but if Jesus Christ the founder of the church should walk into our midst we would fall to our knees.

If Jesus Christ is not the son of God, he is the greatest imposter the world has ever known. If Jesus Christ is only a man, he propagated the greatest fraud known to men. He claimed to be the son of God and all of his claims proved to be true. Listen as he speaks of himself: "I am the truth." "I am the way." "I am the light of the world." "I am greater than Solomon." "I am greater than the temple" "He who has seen me has seen the father." "I am the door." "I am the good shepherd." "I have come down from above." "I have power to lay down my life, and I have power to take it up again." "Come unto me all ye that labour and are heavy laden, and I will give you rest." "Heaven and earth shall pass away but my word shall never pass away." He is the greatest of the great and wisest of the wise. He taught the great greatness and the wise wisdom.

That sermon that Christ preached on the Mount has never died. It has been the wonder and admiration of the greatest minds in all the ages that have intervened. In its profundity, in its suggestiveness, in its simplicity, in its purity of sentiment, in its deep spirituality, in its comprehensiveness, in its majestic sweep, in its practical bearing upon life, it stands unapproached by any thing man has ever uttered or will be able to speak. Socrates said that the teacher that must come must be more than a man that he may teach things impossible for man to know. Jesus Christ was and is that divine person.

JESUS CHRIST IS THE HOPE OF THE WORLD
FOR HE IS THE ONLY TEACHER THAT EVER
PRACTICED TO PERFECTION WHAT HE TAUGHT

Jesus Christ reached the point of perfection in every thing he did. He was as much at ease before the High Court of the Jews and in Pilate's Judgment Hall during his trial as he was on the mountain side while teaching the multitudes. He manifested in a superlative degree everything that was pure, good and holy.

There has never been an original thinker comparable to the Son of God. Matt. 5:27,28:

Ye have heard that it was said by them of old time, Thou shalt not commit adultery: But I say unto you, That whosoever looketh on a woman to lust after her hath committed adultery with her already in his heart.

Jesus Christ as a teacher never hedged, dodged nor side stepped any question: but always faced the issues and placed the emphasis where it belonged. His teaching was so simple and plain that the only ones that misunderstood him were those who closed their eyes and stopped their ears. Anyone who follows in the footsteps of Jesus as a teacher will have no difficulty in making himself known on any doctrinal matter.

Matt. 5:38-39: Ye have heard that it hath been said, An eye for an eye, and a tooth for a tooth: But I say unto you, That ye resist not evil: But whosoever shall smite thee on thy right cheek, turn to him the other also. Matt. 5:43-44: Ye have heard that it hath been said, Thou shalt love thy neighbour, and hate thine enemy. But I say unto you, Love your enemies, bless them that curse you, do good to them that hate you, and pray for them which despitefully use you, and persecute you.

All the educators, intellectual giants and teachers of the world have never given to the world methods of teachings as great as those used by Jesus Christ.

When he wanted to make a contrast between the heavenly and the earthly he said,

> Matt. 6:19-20: Lay not up for yourselves treasures upon earth, where moth and rust doth corrupt, and where thieves break through and steal: But lay up for yourselves treasures in heaven, where neither moth nor rust doth corrupt, and where thieves do not break through nor steal: For where your treasure is, there will your heart be also.

When Jesus made a contrast between two masters he said,

> Matt. 6:24: No man can serve two masters: for either he will hate the one, and love the other; or else he will hold to the one, and despise the other. Ye cannot serve God and mammon.

When he made a contrast with man and the lower animal kingdom he said,

> Matt. 6:26: Behold the fowls of the air; for they sow not, neither do they reap, nor gather into barns; yet your heavenly Father feedeth them. Are ye not much better than they.

When contrasting man's life with the vegetable life he said,

> Matt. 6:28-30: And why take ye thought for raiment? Consider the lilies of the field, how they grow; they toil not, neither do they spin: And yet I say unto you, That even Solomon in all his glory was not arrayed like one of these.

Christ's teaching, as exhibited both in word and deed, is characterized by entire freedom from mistakes. What other teacher ever lived that did not have to amend or take something back that he said? Jesus Christ spoke the absolute and final truth on every subject he discussed.

The sermon on the Mount is just as practical today as it was when spoken by the world's greatest teacher. We need to be preaching it from every mountain top and the people in the valley will hear and many will respond.

Let us observe how he practiced what he taught. Did he practice what he taught concerning the soul? Matt. 16:26: "For what is a man profited, if he shall gain the whole world, and lose his own soul? or what shall a man give in exchange for his soul?" Does his practice agree with his teaching? We see him at Jacob's well. He is talking to a fallen Samaritan woman. A woman who had had five husbands and was living with a man who was not her husband. She was living in such open shame that you and I would hardly dare to recognize or speak to her on the street. When this woman came to Jacob's well to draw water, Jesus, though hungry and thirsty, preached to her one of the most wonderful sermons mortal man ever heard. "The woman then left her water pot, and went her way into the city, and saith to the men, come, see a man, which told me all things that ever I did: is not this the Christ?" How did he value the soul of the adulterous who was brought into his presence. Jn. 8:7: "So when they continued asking him, he lifted up himself, and said unto them, He that is without sin among you, let him first cast a stone at her." Christ also taught, Matt. 5:44: "Bless them that curse you, do good to them that hate you, and pray for them which despitefully use you, and persecute you." Did he practice to perfection what he taught his disciples to do? Lk. 23:34: "Then said Jesus, Father, forgive them; for they know not what they do." There was absolutely no discrepancies between what he taught and what he practiced. Napoleon once compared the life and teachings of Jesus to himself, Caesar, Alexander, Socrates, Plato and others and said, "I know men, and I tell you that the resemblance between Jesus Christ and the founders of great empires and the gods of other religions does not exist." There is between Jesus Christ and all other teachers the distance of infinity. Yes, he practices to perfection everything he taught.

JESUS IS OUR ONLY HOPE BECAUSE
HIS BLOOD CAN CLEANSE US OF OUR SINS

In every continent of the world and on every island of the sea man is conscious of sin. Records dug up from Israel or from the Valley of the Nile show that man has always prayed and cried his heart out because of sin. We are living in an age when the very air that we breathe is reeking with sin we are living in an age when millions have made themselves believe that might makes right. We are living in an age when we see mighty nations attack, destroy and wreak their passions upon weaker ones. We see America so involved in sin that we ask how long will it be before God permits this nation to be destroyed.

God has always destroyed his enemies in every age of the world. In fact, if truth is going to be victorious over error, right over wrong, God over satan, then all of God's enemies must be destroyed. God will only tolerate sin so long. Look at the cities of Sodom and Gomorrah, and remember that God destroyed them. God destroyed Pharaoh's army in the Red Sea. Look at the nations of the world that have fallen because of sin, and remember that America is in all probability one of the most wicked nations of the world. Unless we are able to have enough Christian people who can to some degree hold back this terrible tide of wickedness, God may raise up Red China or Russia to bring America to her knees. The future for America is dark. It could well be that if we knew what the future holds for this country we, no doubt, could go to our rooms and weep and pray all night.

Sin is a violation of God's law, a rebellion against God, a disrespect for law and order and it has almost reached a climax in America. We must remember God cannot overlook sin and be a respectable God. God will not let sin mock him, and it is still an eternal law of life that "The wages of sin is death." Though sin has become socially popular, anyone that believes that it does not carry with it the doom of individual and national calamity is as foolish in his belief as one who could believe that a spider's web could keep a huge boulder from falling down a mountain side. Sin is the most deceptive thing known to men. Sin promises the real thing, and then cheats with the shadow. Sin promises velvet, and then gives in its place a shroud. Sin promises to give liberty, but gives slavery instead. Sin promises silk, but gives sackcloth. Sin promises sleep, but gives a nightmare. Sin promises rest, but gives weariness. Sin is as treacherous as Absalom—doing us obeisance, and at the same time trying to steal our hearts from God. Sin is as deceptive as left handed Ehud, hiding his dagger under his coat, extending his right hand in friendship and using his left hand to plunge the dagger through the stomach. Sin is as hypercritical as Judas, professing love with kisses and soft words, yet eager to betray us unto death. Sin is the eldest born of hell. Sin is worse than the devil for it was sin that made him the devil.

All the prophets of God were conscious of sin and preached about it but they could not take away sin.

Isa. 1:5-6: Why should ye be striken any more? ye will revolt more and more: the whole head is sick, and the whole heart faint. From the sole of the foot even unto the head there is no soundness in it; but wounds, and bruises, and putrifying sores: they have not been closed, neither bound up, neither mollified with ointment.

Isaiah preached about sin, but he could never take away sin. Jeremiah cried his heart out because of sin, but he could not take away sin. Lam. 3:48: "Mine eye runneth down with rivers of water for the destruction of the daughter of my people." The sad truth is that Jeremiah could not take away this sin. John the Baptist was concerned about sin for it seems that the theme of his preaching was repentance. But John, like Isaiah and Jeremiah, could not take away sin.

Even though Isaiah, Jeremiah or John the Baptist could not take away sin, yet we have a blessed hope and that hope is the Lord Jesus Christ. Listen to what authority the Bible speaks concerning Jesus Christ and his ability to take away sin.

Matt. 1:21: And she shall bring forth a son, and thou shalt call his name JESUS: for he shall save his people from their sins. I Jn. 2:2: And he is the propitiation for our sins: and not for our's only, but also for the sins of the whole world. I Jn. 3:5: And ye know that he was manifested to take away our sins; and in him is no sin. I Jn. 4:10: Herein is love, not that we loved God, but that he loved us, and sent his Son to be the propitiation for our sins.

JESUS CHRIST IS OUR HOPE BECAUSE
HE IS THE ONLY ONE GREAT ENOUGH TO SAVE US

Jesus Christ is the only one that can take away sin because he is the only one great enough to do it. He is not only the greatest of the great and the wisest of the wise, but he taught the great greatness and the wise wisdom. Jesus Christ is so great that almost every place he visited became a sacred spot. People from over the world visit what is called the "Holy Land." Why? Well, it is not because of the heavenly character of the people who live there. It is not because of the fertility of the soil or its natural beauty but simply because our Lord lived there. When people visit that land the conversation goes after this order: "It was in this town that he raised the dead. It was in this village that he cast out evil spirit. It was in this community that he healed the daughter of the woman of Canaan. It was at this well that he taught the woman of Samaria the truth about worship. It was in this place where he healed the lepers. It was in this garden where he often went to pray. It was in this mountain where he went to be alone with his Father. It was in this wilderness where he was tempted. It was in this upper room where he instituted the Lord's Supper. It was on this hill where he wept over Jerusalem. It was in this stream where he was baptized and it was out of that cloud that the Holy Spirit descended in the form of a dove." Oh, He is the greatest person the world has ever known.

On one occasion He stood in a little boat and preached to his disciples and that little boat has received more publicity and has been talked about more than any sea going vessel the world has ever been able to build, The Queen Elizabeth or the U. S. S. Enterprise or the Saratoga. Why? Because Jesus Christ stood in that little boat and that made the difference. When He made his triumphant entry into Jerusalem he rode upon a little donkey. That little donkey has been talked about more than the most beautiful Tennessee walking horse or the most graceful Kentucky racehorse or the most elegant stallion of Arabia. Why? Because Jesus Christ rode upon that little donkey.

How does Jesus compare with the great of the earth? Let us imagine a comparison. Someone might have said to him, "I belong to the nobility, I was born in a palace." Christ would have said, "I belong to the peasantry; I was born in a stable." One might have said, "I graduated at Athens, the great university town." Christ would have replied, "I never went to school a day in my life." Can such a man attract men? Can he draw a crowd? Let us observe; "And seeing the multitude, he went up into a mountain." He stands offshore of Galilee to teach them, the crowd is so great that he enters a boat to teach his lesson. He goes into a desert place and great crowds followed him. When he entered a town men left their work to see and hear him. Mothers brought their children to have him lay His hands on them. When He entered Jerusalem men cast branches in the way and shouted, Matt. 21:9 "Blessed is he that cometh in the name of the Lord: Hosanna in the highest." When they would stone him, he passed through their midst, and no man dared to hinder him. Those who crucified him were so impressed as to say, "Truly this was the Son of God." No wonder the prophet said, "His name shall be called Wonderful."